MY FIRST ACTING BOOK

Acting Lessons, Exercises, Tips, and Games for Young Children

MY FIRST ACTING BOOK
Acting Lessons, Exercises, Tips, and Games for Young Children

by Kristen Dabrowski

MY FIRST ACTING SERIES: VOLUME 11

A SMITH AND KRAUS BOOK • HANOVER, NEW HAMPSHIRE

A Smith and Kraus Book
Published by Smith and Kraus, Inc.
177 Lyme Road, Hanover, NH 03755
www.SmithandKraus.com

First Edition: June 2009
Manufactured in the United States of America
9 8 7 6 5 4 3 2 1

ISBN-13: 978-1-57525-605-4 / ISBN-10 1-57525-605-3
Library of Congress Control Number: 2009930163

To my fellow actors and my acting teachers
from around the globe.

CONTENTS

INTRODUCTION

My First Acting Book is for *children* who are curious about what it's like to be an actor; *drama teachers* in schools, theaters, and acting studios; and *parents* who want to know more about getting a child into show business and/or want some new ideas about how to play with kids.

This book is structured into six main parts:

1. Basic Lessons

2. Exercises

3. Professional Tips

4. Games

5. Interviews with Actors and Agents

6. Glossary

My First Acting Book is focused on *how* to act. For kids who are reading this book on their own, feel free to ask an adult for help any time you get confused. For adults reading this book, try the exercises and lessons with children!

When acting is explored with an open mind, a sense of fun, and a quest for adventure, creativity blossoms, understanding and empathy grow, and self-esteem goes through the roof. These ideals, as large as they may be, are the goals of this book. As a child, I was very shy. Performing was a way to "become" other people. It also gave me the skills to overcome my fears. Lastly, acting lent me courage and confidence, which I was able to build upon throughout my life. That's why I think it is an important and enriching skill!

About My First Acting Series

The other books in this series include *My First Monologue Book, My Second Monologue Book, My Third Monologue Book, My First Scene Book,* and *My Second Scene Book.* These books all provide interesting, appropriate, interactive, and fun acting material for children in elementary school. Teachers, if you want to see more, check out the *Teacher's Guide* for this series. Children, once you are done with this book, you may want to check out the rest of the series for monologues and scenes you can act out with your friends. Put your new technique to the test!

If you like what you see, check out the other twenty books I've written. In particular, the 10+ play series has short plays, scenes, and monologues with performance tips, writing ideas, discussion questions after each play, and several games and exploration activities. As always, you are invited to give me comments and ideas and ask questions at monologuemadness@yahoo.com.

Enjoy!

Kristen Dabrowski

BASIC LESSONS

This chapter is all about learning the basics about acting.
Every section has an ACTING MISSION—an exercise challenge
to get you thinking and acting just like a professional actor!

(P.S. You can write in this book or get a special
notebook to draw and write in!)

What is this girl dreaming about?

Big Question 1: WHAT IS ACTING?

Being an actor is all about make-believe.

- Make believe you are somewhere new!
- Make believe you are someone new!
- Make believe you are in another time!

Acting is PRETENDING. Can you pretend you are almost anyone, anywhere, anytime? Of course you can! When you play house or teacher or when you pretend you are in space or the Old West or Hollywood, you are pretending. Do you believe you are a mother, an alien, or a movie star? Yes and no, right? While you are playing, you think, move, speak, and behave like you are the person you are pretending to be. That is *exactly* like acting! Actors don't go home and think they are in a submarine about to sink or that they are living in the year 1732. But while they are acting, they think, move, speak, and behave like they do.

Acting Mission: PRETENDING

Make believe you are a prince or princess during dinner, eating in a castle. Do you feel differently? Do you act differently? Do you eat differently?

Basic
Lessons

2

Big Question 2: HOW DO YOU PRETEND?

Actors need to use their imagination to pretend.

- Even when actors are told what to say and do, imagination helps them pretend they are someone and somewhere new.

- Imagination helps you with everything the script and the teacher/director does not tell you.

Did you use your IMAGINATION to do the last exercise? Imagination is very, very important in acting! It's a big part of pretending, isn't it? You can't blast into the future to the year 2147 or go in a time machine to show what it was like when the dinosaurs walked the earth. Actors always have to use their imaginations to think about who their character is, what he or she is like, and how he or she feels.

Acting Mission: IMAGINATION

Sit in your room. Imagine you are a caveman in your cave.

- What does the cave look like?

- There is a fire burning. Your dinner is being made.

- What do you see, hear, touch, taste, and smell?

- What have you done all day?

- How do you feel now that you are at home, waiting for your dinner?

If you can imagine you are a caveman and your room is your cave, well done. If you were even able to imagine what you smelled, tasted, and touched, super well done! If you were able to *feel* your caveman's emotions, you did an incredible job at imagining.

Basic
Lessons

Big Question 3: HOW DO YOU SHOW WHAT YOU ARE PRETENDING?

When you are an actor, your face and body have to show how you feel.

- Sometimes the feeling can be small, like a smile, or even show only in your eyes.
- Sometimes the feeling needs to be big, like screaming when you think a tree is about to fall on your head!

Actors' voices and bodies show us who they are and what they are thinking and feeling. Just like a piano player uses the piano as an instrument, actors use themselves. So you have to be very aware of your voice and body! Not only does each person have his or her own voice and body, each person's voice and body changes when he or she has a different emotion.

Acting Mission: USING YOUR BODY

Look in the mirror. Look at your eyes. Can you make your eyes look:

Happy?

Sad?

Scared?

Look in the mirror. Look at your feet. Can you make your feet look:

Nervous?

Excited?

Tired?

If you are able to show how you feel even in your feet, you are a very clever actor!

Basic
Lessons

4

Big Question 4: WHAT IS OBSERVATION?

Actors watch behavior, or observe, to learn how to act naturally.

It is important for actors to behave like real human beings. There are lots and lots of ways human beings behave. The way to learn how to behave like someone very different from you is to observe that person.

OBSERVATION is when you watch someone (or something) very closely to see how he or she behaves. How do you use observation in acting? What if you had to pretend to be someone who had only one leg? What if you had to pretend to be someone very old? What if you had to pretend to be someone who has a very different personality from you? It helps actors to observe people who are not like them. This way, their acting is believable and looks real.

Acting Mission: OBSERVATION

Pick someone who is older than you that you know and see a lot. Secretly (like a spy) watch what he or she says and does. When you are alone, see if you can walk and talk like this person.

- Are there any words he or she says a lot? (My second-grade math teacher said he was "cross" when he was angry.)

- Does this person walk faster or slower than you?

- Does this person stick out, push back, turn in or turn out any part of his or her body? (When I was little, I would point my toes in. When I feel stubborn, I stick my chin out a little bit. When I'm thinking or listening, I tilt my head to the side.)

- Does this person act, talk, or walk differently when he or she is happy, sad, or angry?

Here's the trick. You are *not making fun* of this person. Your job as an actor is to try to *be* this person for a little while. If you understand the person you observed a little bit better, you did a great job!

Basic
Lessons

Big Question 5: HOW DO YOU MAKE YOUR VOICE AND BODY WORK TOGETHER?

Your voice and body work together all the time without you knowing it.

How do you sound when you don't want to go to bed? A little whiny? When you say you "don't wanna" go to bed, do you stand up straight and tall or do you slouch and get smaller? When your voice is whiny, your body gets smaller—even your face scrunches up! That's one example of your voice and body working together.

Here's another example. If someone is chasing you when you are playing tag and you scream out, do you use a sudden burst of energy? Does your body feel small or big in that moment? It is hard to scream and yell when your body is floppy like a ragdoll. It hurts your throat!

Acting is just like life. Your voice and your body need to match what you are doing, what kind of character you are playing, and how your character feels. Can you imagine a superhero who had a tiny mouse voice and didn't stand up straight? That superhero wouldn't seem very heroic.

Observe yourself to learn how to make your voice and body WORK TOGETHER. If your body and voice don't match each other, it looks and feels very strange.

Acting Mission:
VOICE AND BODY WORKING TOGETHER

Do what comes naturally and notice what your voice and body do.

- Go outside and call out to someone very far away. What does your voice and body do?

- Tell someone a secret. What does your voice and body do?

- If you get in trouble or you have to apologize to someone, notice what your voice and body do.

- If you don't get to watch a TV show you want to see or if you get sent to bed before you're ready to go, notice what your voice and body do.

If you can remember what your voice and body do after you try these exercises, your observation skills are excellent.

Basic
Lessons

Big Question 6:
HOW DO YOU ACT OUT FEELINGS?

To act out emotions and feelings, you must feel them inside your own body.

Feelings are important for an actor. Why? Because human beings have feelings! When you are acting, you are behaving like a certain human being with a certain life and certain fears and hopes—and all the feelings that go with those things. But do actors have to scream and cry all the time? Well, do you scream and cry all the time? Of course not! Some people show their feelings more than others. But all people have feelings.

Acting is about pretending and believing. Figuring out how your character feels in any situation just means you have to pretend and believe. Everyone has a very good imagination. If you can put yourself into someone else's shoes, you will be a very good actor, and your acting will be real.

Acting Mission: EMOTIONS AND YOUR BODY

Notice your body. When I am frustrated, I feel burning in my stomach and my jaw is tight. When I am scared, I can't keep my feet still and my heart beats fast. See what I mean?

Notice where you feel the following emotions in your body:

Happy

Sad

Excited

Nervous

Frustrated

Angry

Scared

Basic
Lessons

7

Big Question 7: HOW DO YOU BELIEVE?

The more you can make yourself believe new things, the better.

- Believe another actor is your mother or father.

- Believe another actor is your best friend.

- Believe you love mice.

The difference between being an actor and being someone who jokes around and makes fun of people is that actors BELIEVE they are the characters they are playing. Remember, you don't believe you are caveman ten hours after you pretend you are a caveman, but while you are acting, you must believe in who you are, where you are, and what is going on around you.

Can you imagine what it would be like if, in the middle of a movie, an actor turned to the camera and said, "This is all fake! Even the building we are in is fake! This lady who is my wife is just an actress!" Wouldn't that be crazy? If the movie was really good and exciting, that would make me so mad! We count on actors to believe in what they are doing and to act as if everything and everyone around them is real.

Acting Mission: BELIEVING

Lots of times, in TV commercials especially, you have to pretend you like foods that you may not like that much. Next time you have to eat something you don't like, see if you can *act* like you like it! *Believe* it's a food you really like. See if other members of your family are convinced by your acting.

Basic
Lessons

8

Big Question 8: WHAT IS COMMITMENT?

The best actors make us believe everything they do because they believe in everything they do.

- If they are acting for two hours, they believe for two hours.

- If they have to imagine they are about to be swept away by an invisible wave, they completely believe (for that moment) that a wave is about to crash onto them.

- If they have to pretend to be 199 years old, they pretend to be 199 years old, not just 57 years old.

COMMITMENT means putting your whole body and soul into something. When you commit to an imaginary situation as an actor, it means that you believe totally and completely in who you are pretending to be and the situation you are pretending to be in.

Acting Mission: COMMITMENT

Choose one of these situations and act it out:

- You are a servant. You must clean the house (or room or dishes) so there is not a speck of dust on anything. If you don't do this, you will be fired and kicked out of the house, and you have nowhere to go. (You can do this assignment when your parents tell you to clean your room or do chores.)

- You are a professional athlete at the Olympics. You are running in the final race of your career. The doctor told you that your heart is tired and overworked. You should never run again. But you want to win a gold metal, so you run anyway. (You can do this in gym class at school or while playing with your friends.)

How did you feel while you were pretending to be one of these characters? Did you behave differently? Did you have trouble staying committed to your character or the situation? Or was it easy for you to believe and commit?

If you were able to commit and believe in your character and your situation, even for a little while, you succeeded.

Bonus: Make up a new character and situation. See if you can commit for a little bit longer than the last time.

Basic
Lessons

9

Big Question 9:
HOW DO ACTORS WORK
TOGETHER OR COOPERATE?

Actors usually don't act alone. Being able to react to other actors and work as a team is critical.

Sometimes when another person jumps into your imaginary scene, it can make commitment hard! For example, if you were pretending to be a servant in the last Acting Mission (Big Question 8), and your mother walked in and asked how school went, that would make it hard to keep pretending! That's why actors work with other actors when they can. When everyone is pretending to be in the same imaginary time, place, and situation, it makes things a lot easier. To do this well requires COOPERATION.

Acting Mission: COOPERATING

This exercise is called "Yes, and . . ." Here's how it works:

1. Sit with one or more friends or family members. If you have a few people working with you, sit in a circle.

2. One person starts to tell a story. It can be about anything.

3. The second person says, "Yes, and . . . ," then goes on to say the next sentence in the story.

4. The next person says, "Yes, and . . . ," then goes on to say the next sentence in the story—and so on.

Keep going until the story is over or until you just don't know what to say anymore! As much as you can, keep the story sensible, but the most important thing is to agree with what the person before you said, no matter how silly it may be!

Basic
Lessons

10

If you're confused, here's an example of how a story might sound:

PERSON 1: Once upon a time there was a princess who lived in a castle.

PERSON 2: Yes, and her name was Snazzlebee.

PERSON 3: Yes, and she was very beautiful.

PERSON 1: Yes, and she wanted to marry a prince.

PERSON 2: Yes, and there was a prince in the village.

PERSON 3: Yes, and he was married to a dragon.

PERSON 1: Yes, and this made the princess sad.

PERSON 2: Yes, and so she wanted to breathe fire, too.

PERSON 3: Yes, and she went to a magician to get some help.

See? The important thing is not to say "no" or "yes, but." Work together!

Basic
Lessons

Big Question 10: WHAT DOES BEING IN THE MOMENT MEAN?

Being in the moment means paying attention to what is going on right this very second.

Let's look at this tiny scene:

PERSON A: Where are you going?

PERSON B: To the store!

PERSON A: Can I come?

If Person B said her line in an excited way, how would you say the last line? Would you say it like you wanted to go to the store? Like you couldn't wait to get to that store?

If Person B said her line in an angry way, how would you say the last line? Would you say it like you were scared to go with her? Like you were begging to go with her?

See how the way other people behave changes what we do? Actors always have to pay attention to each other and BE IN THE MOMENT. Otherwise, nothing makes any sense!

Acting Mission: BE IN THE MOMENT, PART 1

This is all you have to do: *Really* pay attention to what everyone says to you and how they say it. Make sure you respond to them in a way that makes sense. Be in the moment. That's it!

Here's an example of *not* being in the moment: If my dad asked me if I did my homework, no matter how he asked me, I would always get mad at him. "I'm doing it, OK!" But sometimes he would just ask like he was interested or curious. Other times, he might say it in a really nice way. So the angry way I answered him didn't really make sense. I was not paying attention to him, and that is a big part of being in the moment.

Basic
Lessons

Big Question 11: WHAT IS AN IMPROV?

An improv is a scene you make up as you go, in the moment.

IMPROV is short for improvisation. An improv is a scene with a made-up situation and made-up characters, but it does not have any written lines. In an improv, you don't need to know what anyone else is going to say or do. Your job is to go with the flow and stay committed to your situation and character. There is no right or wrong thing to say or do in an improv unless it doesn't make any sense or you are not in the moment.

Why do actors do improv? Improv forces them to act as a team. If any one person tries to take over, it doesn't work. Also, improv makes you be in the moment. If you don't listen to others or respond to them in a way that makes sense, it doesn't work.

Here are the rules:

- Before you start, decide who everyone is and where everyone is.

- Never say "no" to a partner's idea.

- Always stay in character and be in the moment.

Acting Mission: TRY AN IMPROV

Pick one friend to try this improv out with you. Start the improv with the line, "Look out!" Pretend, believe, and commit to whatever your friend makes up. Observe what the other person says and does very closely. Have fun!

If you managed to do this exercise without disagreeing, arguing, or fighting with each other, you did very well! Were you able to believe what you both made up?

Basic
Lessons

Big Question 12: WHAT IS RESEARCH?

When you look in books and ask experts for information, this is called research.

Sometimes it can be tricky to pretend to be someone else. Sometimes actors can be asked to pretend something they don't know about. For example, actors on TV playing doctors don't really know how to operate on people! So they have to RESEARCH or learn a little bit about what they are pretending so it doesn't look fake.

Acting Mission: RESEARCH

Learn a little bit about a time and place you don't know anything about, like clothing in the seventeenth century (1600–1699). Ask adults or librarians to help. See if you can find at least one picture of what someone wore during this time in history.

Now let's take it one step further, to be more like an actor.

- What do you think it would feel like to wear this clothing?

- Do you think it would change how you move—walking, sitting, standing?

- Would you be rich or poor if you wore this clothing?

- Where do you think you would live? In a house or a shack or a castle?

- Would you be hot in the summertime or cold in the winter?

- Do the clothes look important or glamorous?

- Do the clothes look like something you would wear in the city or the country?

Good job! On to the next step!

Basic
Lessons

Big Question 13:
HOW DO YOU MEMORIZE?

Memorizing is remembering your lines.

Lines are the words actors say that come from the script. The script is a book containing the lines for a play, TV show, commercial, or movie.

Lots of people ask actors, "How do you remember all those words you have to say?" That's a good question. Here are the major ways to make MEMORIZING easier.

- Practice! Repeat the words many, many, many, many, many times.

- Know what is going on (the story of the commercial/play/ TV show/movie).

- Know how your character thinks and feels.

Acting Mission: MEMORIZE

You are an orphan, lost in a new town. Nothing you see looks familiar to you. Your objective is to find your uncle, who owns a shoe factory. You have never met him before, and he is your only relative in the world.

This is your line:

"Where am I? I'll never find my uncle. I don't even know where to look!"

1. Close your eyes and say the line ten times (or until you get it just right).

2. Open your eyes and say the line like you mean it, like you are that orphan.

See, you memorized it!

Bonus: Say the line one more time while also seeing this strange new town for the first time.

Basic
Lessons

Big Question 14:
HOW DO I SAY MY LINES?

Say your lines like you mean them.

Pay attention to the words. Are the words formal ("Good day, sir."), emotional ("How could you do this to me!"), or everyday ("Where's my sock?")?

If you believe you are your character, you will know just how to say your lines. If you aren't sure what a line means, ask the director or the teacher or a grown-up for help. But the most important thing is to say your line like you really, truly mean it. That doesn't mean that everything has to be super-duper emotional and big. If your line is, "Hey, what's up?," it would be strange to say that in a dramatic way. Just SAY IT LIKE YOU MEAN IT.

Acting Mission: SAY IT LIKE YOU MEAN IT

You are doing the voice of a turtle in a cartoon. This turtle is smart and sensible, but his friend, Eric the Rabbit, is always getting him into trouble. Say these lines out loud, like you really mean them:

"Don't go running off again, Eric! You always get us into trouble."

"I guess I'm going to have to fix things again."

"Don't worry about it. It's no big deal."

"Let's go! Before they get back here!"

Basic
Lessons

16

Big Question 15: WHERE DO I GO?

The name for where you move and when is blocking.

BLOCKING, where you move and when, makes watching actors more interesting. If you went to see a play and the characters sat on a sofa the whole time and never moved at all, it would be kind of boring. Blocking should also look real and make sense. If characters in a movie never stopped moving but kept running and darting all over the place, that would be weird, too!

Normally, a director or teacher will give you blocking. You don't have to make it up for yourself. Below are some basic guidelines for performing onstage or in front of a camera.

- Never stand in front of someone else, unless you are told to.

- Never turn your back to the audience or camera, unless you are told to. It's more interesting to watch your face when you talk than to watch your tush!

Acting Mission: BLOCKING

You are the boss of a big company. Sitting in front of you is the laziest person in the office, Melvin.

Below are your lines and your blocking. The blocking is in *italic type*.

> *(Sitting in a chair.)* Melvin, thank you for coming to my office. Where is that report?
>
> Not done? Again?
>
> *(Standing.)* You are fired!
>
> *(Walking to the door and opening it.)* Get out of here. And don't come back!

Do the blocking and say the lines. Take your time. Feel free to practice, hold the book in your hands, and do each step. You can say your lines and do the blocking at the same time after you've practiced a few times.

See how blocking should match how your character feels?

Basic Lessons

17

Big Question 16: WHAT IS MOTIVATION?

Motivation is the reason why you do the things you do.

What motivates you to look out the window during a snowstorm? To see the snow! What motivates you to sit down after you've been playing for a long time? You're tired!

What motivates you to take a bath? Maybe because you're dirty or maybe your mother told you to!

Why would an actor care about motivation? Let's say I'm the director of a play, and I tell you to suddenly scream and run out of the room. I'm guessing you would ask me, "Why?" What you want to know is your MOTIVATION. Without motivation, you would have a lot of people moving around the stage, doing their blocking, for no particular reason—just wandering around. It would look crazy!

Look at the dialogue from the previous Acting Mission (Big Question 15). What is the boss's motivation for standing when he or she says, "You're fired!"?

Acting Mission: BE MOTIVATED

Here are some examples of blocking. You decide what your motivation would be.

- A friend fell off her bike. You call her name and run over to her. Why? What is your motivation?

- Your father does not let you go to a friend's birthday party. You stomp up the stairs and slam your bedroom door. Why? What is your motivation?

- You see smoke coming out of your basement. You scream, rush to the phone, and call the fire department. Why? What is your motivation?

These questions are pretty easy, aren't they? Now you can not only do blocking, you can also figure out your motivation for moving or speaking.

Basic
Lessons

18

Big Question 17: WHAT IS AN OBJECTIVE?

An objective is what you want.

- Actors need to figure out what their characters' want.

- Actors need to show what their characters' want.

- Actors need to believe what their characters' want.

- Actors need to try to get what their characters' want.

I'm going to show you a monologue from the book *My Third Monologue Book* by the amazing writer Kristen Dabrowski (me!). You tell me what Vanessa's OBJECTIVE is (what she wants):

> I didn't do anything wrong. I don't know why I'm in trouble. *He* was bothering *me*!
> Mr. Griswold, please don't call my mom and dad. It wasn't my fault! He was pulling my hair! I know I shouldn't have hit him, but he kept bugging me. Please don't call my parents! I promise I won't ever do it again.
> You *have* to call them? But Billy started it!

What is Vanessa's objective? Does she have more than one objective during the monologue?

Acting Mission: OBJECTIVES

- Think of one objective you have for the future. (Do you want a bike? To be president of the United States?)

- Think of one objective you have right now.

- Think of one objective you have that involves another person. (Do you want your brother/sister to leave you alone? To be allowed to play video games before bed?)

Basic
Lessons

19

Big Question 18:
WHAT IS A RELATIONSHIP?

A relationship is how you are connected to other people.

Everyone has a relationship with everyone else. Do you behave the same way with your teacher as you do with your best friend? Would you act the same way with a stranger as you do with your sister? No way! Knowing the RELATIONSHIP helps us know how to behave. For example, family members and friends are more comfortable together than teenagers on a first date.

In acting, relationships can be brother/sister, parent/child, stranger/stranger, boyfriend/girlfriend—all kinds of things! Actors need to know and show the relationships they are acting out.

Acting Mission: ACTING OUT RELATIONSHIPS

Lots of times as an actor, you have to pretend to know someone really well that you just met. Sometimes, you have to pretend you don't know someone who is your friend. Sometimes you have to pretend not to like someone you do like. Sometimes you have to pretend to love someone you don't love!

With a friend, parent, or brother/sister, try to act out these relationships for one minute each:

- An old couple, married for fifty years, having dinner. Do you like each other? What do you talk about? How do you act around each other?

- A parent telling a teenager to clean his or her room. Does the parent trust the teenager to clean the room? Does the teenager obey or argue? What do you say or do that shows you have known each other for years and years?

- Two strangers sitting next to each other on the bus. Do you look at each other? Do you talk to each other? Do you feel comfortable sitting next to this stranger? How do you show that you've never met before?

If you can commit to acting out each relationship, well done! If you can believe in each relationship for one minute, even if it is *very* different from your relationship with your acting partner, you are growing as an actor!

Basic
Lessons

Big Question 19: WHAT IS AN ACTION?

An action is a step you take to try to get your objective (what you want).

As our objective, let's use the example of wanting to stay up later at night. To get what you want, you might beg ("Please, pleeeeease let me stay up!"), bargain with ("If you let me stay up, I'll throw out the trash every day this week"), or annoy ("I don't wanna, and you can't make me") your parents. To beg, to bargain, and to annoy are all ACTIONS. You do them naturally. But most of us do the same actions over and over.

Sometimes, as an actor, it can help to think about new actions we don't usually use. It can make watching you as a performer more interesting because you're not always doing the same thing.

Acting Mission: ACTIONS

Here are some examples of actions. Match the action with the sentence that shows the action being performed:

Action	Sentence
Alert	Shhh. Take it easy.
Amaze	Watch me turn my eyelid inside out.
Burden	Look out!
Calm	Everything is going to be OK.
Charm	Let me show you my next magic trick!
Comfort	This is all your fault.
Gross out	I like your dress, Mrs. Peterson.

Could you figure out which sentence goes with which action? Fantastic!

Basic
Lessons

21

Big Question 20:
WHAT IS A CHARACTER JOURNEY?

A character journey is how a character changes from the beginning to the end of a story.

Many times, a character learns a lesson or becomes stronger or braver. Of course, if a character is a villain, that character may discover he or she can be defeated! The experience or JOURNEY the character has makes him or her grow as a person.

If characters did not change during a whole play, scene, or movie, it would not be very interesting. And it would be strange! Imagine you crawled for days and days and days across a huge desert. On the way, you ran across many strange people and creatures—some nice, some not so nice. You had to fight to survive. Do you think going through this journey would change you a little bit?

Acting Mission: CHARACTER JOURNEY

Think about a movie you've seen or a story you've read. What did the main character learn? What was his or her journey? How would the character state what he or she learned?

For example, in "Little Red Riding Hood," the character of Little Red Riding Hood might state her journey as follows: "I learned to listen to adults and not to stray from the path because it's not safe. I became braver and smarter after meeting the wolf."

Decide on the journeys for the following characters:

The Wolf in "Little Red Riding Hood":

Jack in "Jack and the Beanstalk":

Dorothy in "The Wizard of Oz":

Big Question 21: HOW DO YOU STAY IN CHARACTER?

When actors completely understand their characters, they know what their characters would do in any situation.

Once you have done your research, imagined what your character is like, observed people like your character, and put your body, voice, heart, and soul into understanding this person, you will know how this person will behave in *any* situation! Isn't that amazing? Then you can act like your character anytime, anywhere, talking to anyone.

Sometimes the script doesn't tell you everything about your character. Whatever you don't know, you need to use your imagination to make up. Unless you do things that don't make any sense, you can't be wrong! Trust yourself.

Sometimes things don't go right during performances, and you must learn to STAY IN CHARACTER—no matter what happens! One time, I walked into a wall by accident in the middle of a play! In these moments, you have to act like your character would or just react like a normal human being would. (Sometimes when actors get nervous, they don't remember to act like they normally would.)

Acting Mission: STAYING IN CHARACTER

Here are a few situations. Decide how you would react.

- You are playing an adult in your own house. A lamp accidentally falls over. What do you do?

- You are playing an evil witch or warlock. You need to cast a spell, but your wand breaks. What do you do?

- You are playing a little boy or girl in a play. You are supposed to leave after another actor says, "Let's go!" But the other actor forgets to say the line. What do you do?

Basic
Lessons

Big Question 22:
HOW CAN ANIMALS HELP US ACT?

Animals act naturally all the time.

Animals behave on instinct. As people, we have to trust our instincts, too. That is one way we can learn from animals.

We can also use animals to help us create new characters or understand characters we are playing. Have you ever seen someone who reminded you of a bird or a walrus or a bulldog? A lot of people resemble animals in big or small ways—not just in how they look, but how they move, talk, and act.

The famous actor Alec Guiness, who played Obi Wan Kenobi in *Star Wars*, always used animals to help him work on his characters.

Acting Mission: ANIMAL STUDIES

Choose the animal you think these characters might act like:

A proud princess would act like _____.

A mighty warrior would act like _____.

A crossing guard who is afraid of cars would act like

_____.

An angry librarian would act like _____.

Create characters that behave like these animals:

Rhino

Hamster

Monkey

Robin

Big Question 23: HOW CAN DOING BORING THINGS HELP US ACT?

When you notice how you do everyday things, it can help you do these activities in a real way when you are acting.

Plays, movies, and TV shows seem a lot more exciting than real life. But watch more closely. Actors performing in plays, movies, and TV shows still wake up, brush their teeth, eat, answer the door, and do all sorts of activities that aren't glamorous. In fact, when you act in commercials, most of the things you do are everyday things.

Many famous acting teachers, like Constantin Stanislavski and Uta Hagen, focus a lot on acting out normal things in a way that isn't phony. Sometimes this can be easy, and sometimes this can be tricky. Lots of times, actors accidentally overact. Overacting is when you make your actions, voice, movements, and emotions too big. When you exaggerate too much, things don't look believable.

Acting Mission: EVERYDAY ACTIVITIES

Observe yourself doing the following activities in real life, then try acting them out in front of someone. Ask that person if he or she thinks you are believable. If not, you probably need to do *less* work to seem more natural.

Doing Homework

Notice how you behave when you do your homework. What do you do when you're thinking? Do you move or stay still? How do you sit when you're writing?

Do ten math problems in front of an audience of friends or family members (two or more people, if you can). Tell them it might be very boring to watch, but the audience's job is to tell you afterwards if your behavior looked real and normal. Were there any moments when you were overacting (making your actions or emotions too big)? If so, try it again another day!

Basic
Lessons

Waking Up

Take your time getting up in the morning. Notice each thing you do. Do your eyes pop right open, or do you need a few minutes to open them up all the way? What is your breathing like? What parts of your body move first? Are your movements slow or fast?

Now try acting out "waking up in the morning" for family members, especially someone who sees you wake up in the morning. Do they think you are acting the same as you do in real life? Why or why not?

Tip: If you didn't seem natural yet, try doing *less* work and making your movements slower and more relaxed. Actors sometimes overdo their actions and move too quickly when people are watching them because they get nervous or excited.

These are difficult missions. If you successfully complete them, you are a very accomplished actor. Grown-up actors do these same things!

Basic
Lessons

Big Question 24: HOW DO YOU PRETEND NOT TO KNOW THE END?

Remember, when you act, lots of times you know *exactly* how a story will end and *exactly* what will happen. But you need to pretend that you don't know the ending! Your character doesn't know that there's a wolf in the woods or that he or she is about to find a time machine.

Think about your favorite movie, TV show, or play. Imagine what it would be like if the characters acted like they knew the ending. Would they be scared all the time? Would they be relaxed even when dangerous, scary, or sad things were happening because they knew everything would be OK in the end? Wouldn't that be boring and strange? Those actors would not be acting in the moment. And the audience might be able to tell what was going to happen instead of being surprised.

Actors Mission: BE IN THE MOMENT, PART 2

Have a friend or family member hide a homework assignment in your room. Imagine this is something you really, really need *right now*. If you don't find this homework assignment *now*, you are going to get in big trouble—you'll fail the class and get yelled at. You *must* find it! Look for the lost item. (If you can't find it after looking really hard for it, ask your friend or family member to tell you where they hid it.)

This is a tough mission! Now hide the item yourself. Then ask your friend or family member to be your audience (quietly watching). Act out trying to find your homework assignment as if you have no idea where it could be. (Remember, if you don't find it, you will be in big trouble.) When you are done acting (when you "find" the homework assignment), ask your friend or family member if it looked like you really were looking for what you lost. Was your acting natural and believable?

Basic
Lessons

Big Question 25:
WHAT ARE WORKING ACTIONS?

Working actions are eight different ways of moving that can help with voices, movements, and feelings.

Here are the WORKING ACTIONS:

Punching Floating Wringing Gliding

Pressing Dabbing Slashing Flicking

The best way to learn about working actions and how they can help your acting is just to try them out. Let's go right to the mission!

Acting Mission: WORKING ACTIONS

Find a place where you can be by yourself and have some room to move around without bumping into anything. Try a few of the working actions and see how they make you feel:

- **Punching.** Punch the air like you're a boxer. Be strong and quick with your movements. How do you feel inside? Can you keep your hands still and talk like you're punching? What does a punching voice sound like? Can you feel like you're punching inside?

- **Wringing.** Get a towel. Twist and twist and twist it. Imagine the towel is soaking wet and you need to get all the water out of it. How do you feel when you're wringing? How does your back feel when you're wringing? How does your jaw feel? Can you put the towel down and talk like you're wringing? What emotions do you feel when you're wringing? What kind of person might feel like he or she is wringing inside all the time?

- **Floating.** Floating is light, steady, and wanders in all directions. Try floating around the room. How does this make you feel? What kind of person might be a floating person? Can you talk in a floating way? How does floating make you feel?

When you can figure out what working action your character does the most, it can help you create the character. A character might have different working actions for different situations. For example, a character could be a slashing person most of the time (like cutting through bushes in the jungle) but glide when he or she is happy.

Basic
Lessons

28

Big Question 26: HOW DO YOU GET PROFESSIONAL ACTING JOBS?

To get work as an actor, you may need some help.

An actor can perform in lots of places—at school, at camp, in acting or singing classes, in a choir, in community theater (a theater group near your house): there are lots of possibilities! Professional jobs are acting jobs you get paid to do. They can be in theater, commercials, TV, or the movies.

Agents and Managers. Agents and managers can help you get jobs. They both get paid by actors after they help them get a job.

An agent finds auditions for actors. The agent also helps actors get paid after they get a job.

A manager helps actors pick the best jobs for them. The manager also helps organize actors.

(For more information about how to get professional acting jobs, see the "Professional Tips" chapter.)

Casting Directors. An audition is a tryout for an actor. Usually the actor reads some lines or does a monologue.

A casting director decides which actors get the jobs. A casting director can also call actors to come in for auditions.

Note: Never, never, never pay someone unless they help you get professional acting work.

Acting Mission: SHOWBIZ

Find out if there are any community or children's theaters near you. If you can, go see one of their shows!

Basic
Lessons

Big Question 27: WHAT IS AN AUDITION?

In an audition, an actor tries out for a part in a play, TV show, movie, or commercial.

Actors go to AUDITIONS to get work. At the audition, they read lines or perform a monologue or a scene while pretending to be a character.

Acting Mission: FIND A MONOLOGUE

Find a monologue you like. A good place to look is *My First Monologue Book, My Second Monologue Book,* or *My Third Monologue Book,* all published by Smith and Kraus and written by me! Then turn to "Working on Monologues and Songs" on page 54 for advice on how to perform a monologue.

Practice acting out the character. See if you can memorize the monologue! Perform it for a friend or family member.

Basic
Lessons

Big Question 28:
WHAT DO YOU WEAR TO AN AUDITION?

Actors need to look nice for an audition. But they do not wear costumes until they are in the play!

An actor shouldn't be too dressed up at an audition. An actor also shouldn't look sloppy! You should look like yourself, too. You don't need makeup or a hairstyle that takes four hours to do.

Acting Mission: CHOOSING AN OUTFIT

Which outfit is best for a boy actor going on an audition?

Suit and tie

Cowboy outfit

Sweatpants and a ripped T-shirt

Nice pair of pants and a clean shirt

Cow costume

Which outfit is best for a girl actor?

Tutu

Hobo costume

Nice pair of pants or a skirt and a clean shirt

Ballgown

Pajamas

If you can't figure out the answers to these questions—eeeek! You are smart enough to know that you need to look nice and neat, but like yourself.

Basic
Lessons

31

Big Question 29: HOW SHOULD ACTORS BEHAVE WHEN THEY ARE NOT ACTING?

Would you want to talk to someone who is mean or rude? No one does! Actors need to act nicely and politely, just like everybody else, even if they are rich and famous.

Acting Mission: GREETING YOUR PUBLIC

One day when you are at school, imagine you are famous. Everyone knows you. See how many people you can smile at and say hello to. Be a role model for younger children!

Write down five nice things you did today:

1. _____

2. _____

3. _____

4. _____

5. _____

Basic
Lessons

32

Big Question 30: ARE LOTS OF ACTORS RICH AND FAMOUS?

Most actors are *not* rich or famous. Most actors perform because they love to. They love becoming other characters. They love the applause at the end of the show. They love imagining how other people think and feel.

Acting Mission: DO YOU LOVE ACTING?

What do you think you might love about acting, even if you were not rich or famous?

What would be the best part in the world to play?

Who would you like to imagine being?

Where would you like to go (for real or in a play/TV show/movie)?

What costume would you like to wear?

Basic
Lessons

EXERCISES

Try these ideas out one or two at a time. Ask for help from a family member or teacher if you need it. See if you can get a friend or two to do the exercises with you!

What exercise do you think this boy is doing?

WARM-UPS

Why do a warm-up?

Often actors need to move quickly or dance. Also, in large theaters, actors need to project (speak up so they can be heard even far away). Warm-ups keep actors from hurting their bodies and their voices when they rehearse or perform.

Voice Only

Stretches and Sounds

Try these!

- Stretch your face out wide, making everything as big as possible.

- Scrunch your face up very tightly like an angry old man.

- Pretend to chew an enormous piece of bubble gum, moving your lips all around.

- Stick your tongue out as far as it will go.

- Hum on an "m"—see if you can make your lips itch (that's good!). Try different pitches, make your pitch higher and lower.

- Change to a "v" sound—see if you can make your lower lip itch. Try different pitches, make your pitch higher and lower.

- Change to a "w" sound—see if you can feel vibrations in your cheeks. Try different pitches, make your pitch higher and lower.

- Change to a voiced "th" sound like "that"—see if you can make your tongue itch. Try different pitches, make your pitch higher and lower.

- Put your lips together and try to roll a "b"—like a helicopter sound! Try different pitches, make your pitch higher and lower.

- Quack like a duck; make the sound go into your nose. Try different pitches, make your pitch higher and lower.

Exercises

Mega Tongue Twisters

Pick one or two of the following tongue twisters. Try saying them through slowly a few times, then speed up. See if you can say them five times in a row without messing up!

Tip: It helps to move your mouth and tongue around a lot.

Three free throws.

A box of biscuits, a batch of mixed biscuits.

Mrs. Smith's Fish Sauce Shop.

Six thick thistle sticks. Six thick thistles stick.

Unique New York.

Toy boat, toy boat, toy boat.

Knapsack straps.

The myth of Miss Muffet.

Fat frogs flying past fast.

Shy Shelly says she shall sew sheets.

Body Only

Shake, Rattle, and Roll

Put on some fast music. Shake and wiggle in one spot until you feel loose, warm, and energized!

Put on some slower music with no words and see if you can move in new and unusual ways. Here are some ideas:

- Walk as if you are on the moon.
- Swim through a big room filled with caramel!
- Dance like a fairy.
- Crawl like the world's biggest bear.

Body and Voice Together

Move, Speak, Be

Pick a sentence with some interesting sounds or an interesting idea. Here are a few:

How the wild winds blow!

The Queen is on her way!

Where in the world can we be?

Say your sentence in as many different ways as possible. Say it loud, say it soft; imagine you are in a castle, imagine you are in a muddy hut; say it high, say it low; imagine you are someone wealthy, imagine you are someone poor.

While you are imagining different things and saying your sentence in different ways, move your body in ways that help what you are doing. If you are imagining you are a king speaking loudly, make your body big and strong, too! If you are a mouse who is scared, make your body quick and small.

Now that your voice and body are warmed up, you can move on to an advanced warm-up, exercises, or rehearsing!

Exercises

VOICE GAMES

Try speaking in new ways and see how it makes you feel and act differently. These are great exercises to help you find a character's voice.

Resonance

- Try focusing the sound on your lips.

- Try talking through your nose (very nasal).

- Make your vowel sounds longer and fuller (vowels: A, E, I, O, U).

- Spit out the consonants (consonants: all the other letters, like C, D, F, G, H).

Rhythm

- Talk like a machine gun.

- Talk like you're very, very relaxed.

- Mix up rhythms. What works for your character?

Pitch

- Make your pitch higher, even squeaky.

- Make your pitch low and deep.

- Move your pitch up and down. What works for your character?

Cartoon Voices

- Try talking in a bunch of silly, weird voices. Experiment! Can you come up with a new, unique, weird, unusual voice?

- Try at least five new ways of talking.

Echo

- Pick a partner and stand on opposite sides of the room. Say a line and have your partner repeat what you said. Can your partner hear and understand you? Are you projecting your voice?

- Think about sending your voice out in an arc. Put your whole body into what you are saying. Have a strong desire to tell the other person in the room your line.

- Pretend to throw a baseball and say a line at the same time. Can you throw your voice as far as you throw that baseball?

Exercises

BODY GAMES

Try moving in new ways and see how it makes you feel and act differently. These are great exercises to help you find a character's way of moving.

Character Walks

Use Emotions

Walk across the room in character while saying a line from the play.

Do the above, but change the emotion to joy.

Do the above, but change the emotion to sadness.

Do the above, but change the emotion to anger.

Do the above, but change the emotion to fear.

Questions

- How does your walk change when the emotion changes?
- How does your voice change when the emotion changes?
- Are you able to stay in character?
- Did you learn something new about your character by trying a new emotion?

Use New Environments/Situations

Walk across the room in character, while saying a line from the play.

Do the above, but imagine you just won a million dollars.

Do the above, but imagine you have to go to the bathroom.

Do the above, but imagine you are lost in the woods.

Do the above, but imagine you just landed on a tropical island.

Do the above, but imagine you just got home from a long trip.

Questions

- How does your walk change when the situation changes?
- How does your voice change when the situation changes?
- Did you learn something new about your character?

Exercises

QUIET WORK

If you already have a part in a play, TV show, or movie, fill in this worksheet to understand more about the play and your character. Have fun! Make up anything you do not know, as long as it makes sense.

Plot

Write down what this play is about! What are the main things that happen to your character?

This play is about _____
_____
_____.

The main things that happen to me are _____
_____
_____.

Character Journey

Does your character learn anything by the end?

I learned _____
_____
_____.

Objective

What does your character want? Does he or she want more than one thing?

I want to _____.

I want to _____.

I want to _____.

Exercises

CHARACTER BIOGRAPHY

Who is your character? Try doing this worksheet, pretending you are your character.

Name: _____

Age: _____

Height: _____

Weight: _____

Job (if you have one): _____

Where you live: _____

Family (brothers, sisters, parents): _____

_____

Favorites

Food: _____

Song: _____

Movie: _____

Place: _____

Book: _____

Animal: _____

Smell: _____

Subject in school: _____

Sound: _____

Person: _____

Exercises

42

Circle all the words that describe you:

Shy	Friendly
Leader	Follower
Neat	Messy
Funny	Calm
Smart	Lazy
Sneaky	Honest
Creative	Kind
Happy	Sad
Curious	Careful
Dramatic	Brave
Strong	Quiet
Lucky	Unlucky

Answer these questions as your character:

I'm really scared of: _____

If I could have any job in the world, I'd: _____

Superpower I'd most like to have: _____

I'm best at: _____

I'm not very good at: _____

My biggest, deepest, darkest secret is: _____

Exercises

43

THE FIVE SENSES (PLUS ONE)

Noticing your senses—how you experience and sense what is going on around you—is very important for an actor. The five senses are seeing, hearing, smell, taste, and touch. I added speaking, which is not a sense, but as an actor, it is also important to pay attention to what you say and what is said to you.

Think about what your character is seeing, hearing, smelling, tasting, touching, and saying.

What do you SEE?

What do you HEAR?

What do you SMELL?

What do you TASTE?

What do you TOUCH?

What do you SAY?

What is SAID TO YOU?

What is SAID ABOUT YOU?

Exercises

ACTING EXERCISES FOR TEACHERS

What's in a Box?

Objective: To use the body and imagination in new ways.

1. Students sit in a circle.

2. Each person has an imaginary box in front of him or her.

3. Silently, students open their boxes to see what is inside.

4. Without using their voices, one at a time, students show the class what is in their box. Can the class guess what they have without being told? Model an example: How can you show it's a hammer? Or a cat?

Who Am I?

Objective: To use voice and body to show character.

1. Students sit in a group and pick a character from a hat (cheerleader, director, wrestler, one-hundred-year-old man). Emphasize that they need to act out the character they pulled out of the hat even if that character is very different from them. We are acting!

2. One at a time, students walk through the door pretending to be their characters—using their voices and bodies, but not saying who they are.

3. The class guesses who they are. If it's a tough one, the teacher can ask questions to help ("Do you go to school?" "Do you like sports?" "Is it hard for you to walk up stairs?" "Do you like to tell people what to do?").

King's/Queen's Court

Objective: To use voice and body to show character.

1. Students sit in a group.

2. One person (or the teacher) is chosen to be King or Queen. That person must act grand and important, like a queen or king.

3. All the other students choose animals to be—but don't tell anyone what their animals are.

4. One by one, students act out their animals. Other students guess what the animal is. (If it's hard, the King/Queen may ask five questions to help figure it out.)

5. If the animal is guessed, the King/Queen puts the animal on his or her court (sitting beside the King/Queen) and declares him or her a Knight, Prince, Princess, and so on.

6. If a student's animal is not guessed, he or she tries again with a new animal.

Locomotion

Objective: To work as a group, using voices and bodies.

1. Students stand in a large circle.

2. One person goes into the center of the circle and makes sounds and movements like a train.

3. One by one, the other students join in, doing their own sounds and movements. (The teacher chooses who goes into the circle and when.) Each person should make his or her own unique sound and movement.

By the end, you should have a magnificent train—though it may not look or sound like a traditional train. Praise creative and imaginative teamwork!

Variation: Try the exercise again with another subject (for example, the ocean). Encourage students to work with other students and explore different sounds and movements.

You're Copying Me!

Objective: To pay attention to others, to be spontaneous, to behave out of character, to bond as a group.

1. Students stand in a circle.

2. Taking turns, each person does a unique movement or gesture with a unique sound

3. After each person's movement/sound, everyone in the group must copy him or her

Tell the students to not think before doing their movements and sounds; they should do whatever pops into their minds first!

See It/Repeat It

Objective: To pay attention to others and observe closely, to be spontaneous.

1. Students stand in two lines facing each other. The person standing directly across from them is their partner.

2. Taking turns, each person says one factual thing about his or her partner. (For example, Partner 1: "You have brown eyes." Partner 2: "You have long hair.") They go back and forth a few times. (Discourage any positive or negative comments—just the facts.)

Tell students that if they can't think of anything to say, to repeat what their partners said. For example, if one student says, "You have red shoes," the other student replies, "I have red shoes." But they must not add any new information! Tell them to keep their focus on their partners.

To Increase Difficulty

After students understand the concept, challenge them to speed up their responses. Ask them to say the first thing that comes to mind and not take time thinking up replies.

To increase the difficulty even more, tell students to notice their partners' behavior in the moment—while it's happening. This also makes the exercise fun and fast.

Discourage students from talking about themselves in the exercise. This exercise is especially good for students who dominate or demand attention as it requires them to observe others.

Hints: Switch partners frequently. Have someone on the left end of one line walk to the right end of the line and have the rest of the students shift over to the left.

Exercises

47

ACTIONS

An action in the acting world is an active verb used to describe the tactics you take to get your objective. The action does not describe your internal feelings but is what you do to change your partner's behavior. Fill in the following sentence with a word from the list below.

To get my objective, I will 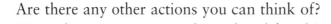 my partner.

Agitate	Embarrass	Pester
Alert	Embrace	Please
Amaze	Empower	Poke
Astonish	Encourage	Press
Bewitch	Entice	Provoke
Boost	Fascinate	Pull in
Brighten	Flatten	Pump up
Burden	Flatter	Push away
Calm	Force	Rattle
Captivate	Gladden	Redirect
Caution	Gross out	Relax
Charm	Guilt	Repulse
Cheer Up	Impress	Scare
Comfort	Inspire	Shock
Console	Irritate	Strengthen
Cool Down	Jolt	Subdue
Dare	Manipulate	Tease
Depress	Nurture	Tickle
Discourage	Outrage	Toy with
Distract	Overwhelm	Wind up
Dominate	Pamper	Worry

Are there any other actions you can think of?

Now, choose a partner and stand and face him or her. Without touching your partner, say words or act in a way that makes your partner respond with the action you have chosen. For example, if I wanted to CALM my partner, I might say, "Everything is going to be OK!" If I wanted to GROSS OUT my partner, I might pick my nose! The partner's job is to observe and react naturally until it is his or her turn to try out an action.

To the Teacher

Before you begin, ask students to choose a line from a monologue or scene and say it out loud.

Ask students how this exercise might help when acting in a play. By thinking about actions, does it help you know how to act? What else does it do? Do you pay more attention to the other actors?

At the end, ask students to say their lines again, thinking of an action. How is it different than when you started?

Note: This is a good warm-up at the beginning of each class. Students learn new words, pay attention, have fun, and gain mastery quickly.

REHEARSAL GAMES FOR
TEACHERS/DIRECTORS

Here are some things to try if you need to freshen things up at rehearsals.

- Do a speed-through of lines.

- Do a loud-through of lines.

- Do a speed-through of blocking.

- Do an opposite-through—playing characters the *opposite* of how you think they should be played. See if you make any new discoveries.

- Do a paraphrase-through of the lines. Do you know what happens next? Do you know your character's true intention in each scene? Can you say the real lines with as much feeling as you say the paraphrased lines?

Exercises

PERFORMANCE PARTY GAMES FOR PARENTS AND KIDS

- **Favorite Song.** Sing and act out your favorite songs with friends. Play air guitar and use something in the house to be your microphone (but not something pointy like a fork, knife or pencil!).

- **Scenes from a Movie.** Act out a scene from your favorite movie or TV show.

- **Sensory Game.** Find items in the house that feel and smell different from each other and that you can put in your hand. Have everyone put on a blindfold and pass each item around. See if you can guess what each thing is without looking at it!

- **The Crown.** It is hard to be a King or a Queen. Everyone always wants to take your job. This game shows you what it's like while having fun! One person sits on a chair wearing a crown and a blindfold. Starting from the other side of the room, everyone else tries to sneak up on the King or Queen and take the crown off his or her head. If the King or Queen hears a noise, they strongly point toward the sound. Whoever gets pointed at must go back to the starting point.

- **Guessing Games.** See "Who Am I" and "Queen's Court" on page 45.

- **Life On/In/As.** Make up different places to live and different kinds of people. Here are some examples: Life on the Moon, Life in the Desert, Life in 1232, Life as a Giant, Life in Heaven. Give everyone one minute to act out each of these people, places, and times.

- **A Picture's Worth a Thousand Words.** Everyone stands in two lines on opposite sides of the room. One person is the photographer and calls out a picture he or she wants to see, such as the circus, going to the dentist, swimming underwater, or superheroes. Everyone else strikes a pose (on their own or with others) that acts out the "picture." The photographer counts down "three, two, one" and takes a picture. Then the game starts again with a new photographer calling out for a new image to be acted out.

- **Park Bench.** Choose a sofa or a few chairs to be the "park bench." One person sits on the park bench pretending to be a totally normal, everyday person. Another person plays a wacky stranger who tries any way he or she can to get the normal person off the park bench (barks like a dog, pretends to be an alien, sneezes on the normal person). Whatever the wacky stranger chooses to do, the normal person MUST get off the bench. Take

Exercises

turns pretending to be the normal person and the wacky stranger. See how many different actions you can try to get the person off the bench!

- **Improv Story.** Everyone sits in a circle and picks a word out of a hat. The words can be weird or normal (hat, alligator, icicle). Someone starts a story using the word he picked. The next person in the circle continues the story, using the word she chose. Let's say the first person picked the word "chicken." He could say, "Once upon a time, there was a prince who loved to eat chicken with sweet and sour sauce." If the next person has the word "garbage," she might say, "One day the prince saw chicken with sweet and sour sauce in the garbage."

- **Guess the Leader.** This is an observation game and a game for working together. Everyone sits in a circle. One person is chosen to be the Guesser and leaves the room. Another person is then chosen to be the Leader. The Leader carefully leads the group, clapping or moving his or her hands. The group's job is to follow the Leader so well that it's hard to figure out who the Leader is. After a minute of the group working together, the Guesser is called back into the room to try to guess who the Leader is. (*Hint:* It makes it harder if everyone does not stare at the Leader!) Take turns playing the Guesser and the Leader.

Exercises

PROFESSIONAL TIPS

Want to be an actor?
Here are some things you need to know!

What do you think these actors are saying to each other?

WORKING ON MONOLOGUES AND SONGS

Monologues

What is a monologue?

A monologue is an acting piece with only one person talking. There may be other imaginary characters around, but we only hear what one person has to say.

A good monologue contains some kind of problem or issue so it is interesting to watch.

When do you use a monologue?

Monologues are mostly used for classes and for auditions (when you try out for a part in a play).

What kind of monologue works best?

A monologue should be:

- Short!

- Right for your age

- Right for your looks

- Something you like to perform

- Right for the role you audition for

Tip: You should have two monologues ready for auditions—one that is serious (dramatic) and one that is funny (comic).

How do you work on a monologue?

Step 1: Understand the monologue. The first step is to understand your monologue. Here are some basic questions to ask:

- Who is the person speaking?

- How old is this person?

- Where is this person? At home, in the mall, in school?

Professional
Tips

- To whom is this person speaking? To the audience or to another character we do not see?

- Why does this person need to speak right now? What is the problem?

- How does this person feel?

- Does another character speak (even though we don't hear him or her)?

Below is a monologue from *My First Monologue Book*. The character's name is Joe. Joe just finished playing a board game with his family. He lost.

I hate losing! You cheated! This game is stupid. I don't care if I broke the game board.

I don't see why *she's* crying; *I'm* the one who lost this stupid game. You have no reason to be upset! I'm never, ever playing this game again!

Don't worry. I'm already going to my room. It's better than being here.

Read the monologue carefully, then answer these questions:

- Who is Joe?

- How old do you think Joe is?

- Where is Joe?

- What is happening before the monologue starts?

- What is the problem? What happened to Joe?

- How is Joe feeling in this monologue?

- Why is he feeling that way?

- When Joe says, "I don't see why she's crying," who is "she"?

- What is going on around Joe?

- Who is Joe talking to?

- What does Joe's mother or father say to him at the end of the monologue?

Step 2: Memorize the words. Practice, practice, practice! Work on it with your family or friends to try to remember all the words without looking. This is called memorizing. When all the words are memorized, then the real fun starts!

Professional
Tips

Step 3: Imagine the scene. Picture everything in the scene.

- What the room looks like

- Where everyone is sitting

- Whether you are sitting or standing

Remember, the audience wants to see your face, so put all the other characters in front of you. Don't make any of them too short so you aren't looking at the ground.

For Joe's monologue, you might imagine yourself in a living room with a sofa and a coffee table. You could picture your father and mother sitting on the sofa and your crying sister standing in a corner of the room. Because you're angry, you might be standing.

Practice saying the monologue to these imaginary people in the room. When do you look at your sister? When do you talk to your parents?

Step 4: Say it with feeling. Once you understand the monologue, can remember all of the words, and can picture the setting, add in the very best part—feelings! When you rehearse (practice), try saying your monologue to other people. How do they feel listening to you? How do you feel saying the words? It sometimes helps to think that the imaginary people in the room (the sister and parents in the Joe monologue) have a hard time understanding you. You must explain to them how you feel and what you think!

Songs

Working on songs is just like working on a monologue. There is one more step: Learn the tune to the song! Sometimes you may have to learn a dance, but if you are auditioning for a part with a song, the important thing is to understand WHAT you are saying, WHY you are saying it, and HOW it makes you feel.

Professional
Tips

WORKING ON SCENES

What is a scene?

A scene is an acting piece with more than one person talking. A good scene contains some kind of problem or issue so it is interesting to watch.

When do you use a scene as an actor?

Scenes are used all the time—for auditions and in classes, plays, TV shows, and movies

What kind of scene works best?

A scene should be:

- Right for your age (so you can understand it)
- Something you like to perform

How do you work on a scene?

Step 1: Understand the scene. The first step is to understand your scene. Here are some basic questions to ask:

- Who is in the scene?
- How old is each person?
- Where does the scene take place? At home, in the mall, in school?
- What problem is happening right now?
- How does each person feel?

One the next two pages is a scene from *My First Scene Book* called "The Deep End." Read and study it and then answer the questions that follow it.

Professional
Tips

57

(PENNY is in her bathing suit. FRED, the lifeguard, enters.)

FRED: OK, Penny. For your swimming lesson today, you are going to get into the deep end of the pool.

PENNY: The deep end?

FRED: Yes. You've been practicing for a long time. You are ready.

PENNY: I don't think I'm ready.

FRED: You remember how to tread water?

PENNY: A little.

FRED: How to float on your back?

PENNY: I guess so.

FRED: How to do the doggy paddle?

PENNY: I'm not that good at it.

FRED: You're ready. Come on. Let's go!

PENNY: Could we just do another day by the steps?

FRED: Penny, I promise I'll be right there to help you if you get in trouble. But you are a good swimmer now! You shouldn't worry.

PENNY: I think I need more practice.

FRED: I'm the teacher, Penny. I think you are ready!

(PENNY thinks for a minute, unsure about what to do.)

PENNY: I don't know.

FRED: Look, your dad is right over there. He believes you can do it. I believe you can do it!

PENNY: I don't know. I'm just—I don't think I want to.

FRED: Why not?

PENNY: I just . . . I don't think I want to.

FRED: Are you scared?

PENNY: No! I mean . . . maybe.

FRED: I told you that I would be right there with you. Would I let you drown?

PENNY: I don't know.

FRED: You think I'd let you drown, right in front of me?

Professional
Tips

(PENNY starts to smile.)

PENNY: No. I guess not.

FRED: Just try it. Try it once. We'll stay in the deep end for five minutes, then come back to the shallow end by the steps.

PENNY: I like it by the steps. Then if I swallow water, I can get out fast.

FRED: I know. But sometimes you have to take risks.

PENNY: Why?

FRED: If you only did what felt easy to you all the time, well, you'd just sit around watching TV all day!

PENNY: That sounds good!

FRED: No, it doesn't, Penny. That might be fun for a little while, but you would get bored.

PENNY: I don't think I would. I like TV.

FRED: Think about all you would be missing! You wouldn't meet any new people. You wouldn't see snow or flowers or grass—

PENNY: I could look out the window.

FRED: Penny, I promise you it's good to scare yourself a little bit sometimes. Especially when it is safe. And I promise you that you will be safe. Come on, let's just try. Will you try for me, Penny?

PENNY: Well . . .

(DAD enters.)

DAD: I'm so proud of you, Penny. Fred says that you are going to go into the deep end of the pool today! I never learned to swim, and I always regretted it. Once, I got invited to spend a summer with my friend Jack, but I told my mother I didn't want to go. I was scared to go because I couldn't swim. I always was sad that I didn't get to go to the beach with Jack that summer. That is why I want you to learn how to swim.

(PENNY takes a long, deep breath.)

PENNY: OK, Fred. I'm ready. I think.

FRED: Let's go into the deep end!

DAD: You're a brave girl, Penny!

Professional
Tips

59

After you've read the scene carefully, answer these questions:

- Who are the characters?
- How old do you think the characters are?
- Where is the scene taking place?
- What is the problem?
- How does Penny feel in this scene?
- How does Fred feel in this scene?
- How does Dad feel in this scene?
- What happens at the end?

Step 2: Memorize the words. The next step is to practice, practice, practice. Work on it with your family or friends to try to remember all the words without looking. An actor needs to memorize all the lines he or she says plus the "cues." A cue is the line that comes right before your line. If you don't know your cue, you won't know when to say your line!

Step 3: Add props and blocking. Walk through the scene and add simple costumes or props. Work out the blocking.

- Where should each person stand so he or she can be seen?
- Does anyone enter or exit during the scene?
- Do the characters sit or stand?
- Does anyone need to hold anything or have a special costume? Keep it simple and don't add too much!

To use "The Deep End" as an example, I would have all the characters stand. Dad comes in toward the end of the scene after Penny says, "Well . . ." To keep the costumes and props simple, I would imagine that this scene takes place *before* Fred and Penny change into their bathing suits. Maybe they would both carry a towel and Fred would have a whistle around his neck, like a lifeguard.

Remember, the audience wants to see your face and hear what you have to say. Don't turn your back to the audience, especially if you are talking.

Step 4: Add feeling. Once you understand the scene, can picture the setting, and remember all the words in the right places, add in the very best part—feelings! When you rehearse (practice), pay attention to other actors in the scene. How do they feel? How do you feel? Do they understand you? Can you make them believe what you are saying?

Professional
Tips

60

QUICK TIPS: BEING AN ACTOR

Where to Start

- Who am I?

- Where am I?

- Who am I talking to?

- Why am I here?

- What is going on?

- How do I feel about what is going on and who I am talking to?

Pay close attention to the other person in the scene. Listen. Watch. Respond to them. Act the way you think your character would act in this situation. Remember it's all imaginary and have fun pretending.

Working on Songs

- Act out the song.

- Choose something you love to sing.

- Choose something that is right for the musical.

- Choose something right for your age.

Professional
Tips

WORKING WITH A DIRECTOR

A director is a person who is in charge of a play or movie. They are responsible for telling actors where to go and how they want them to behave in a scene. Here are some rules for working with a director.

Rules

Do

1. Make suggestions. ("What if I tried doing _____?")

2. Give ideas. ("I have an idea! What if we made my character very old?")

3. Ask questions. ("What does this word mean?")

4. Think about how to use your voice and your body.

5. Listen.

6. Watch.

7. Be open to the ideas the director gives you.

8. Praise your partner when he or she does well!

9. Speak respectfully.

10. Be helpful.

11. Cooperate!

Don't

1. Demand. ("Do it my way!")

2. Boss around. ("I said to do it like this!")

3. Be negative. ("No, no! That's all wrong.")

4. Insist on getting your way. ("Do it the way I said.")

5. Get mad at your partner.

6. Tell your partner how to say their lines.

Your job is to act out the director's and the playwright's ideas. The key is to be open to trying things different ways and to not be stubborn or get stuck. Have fun!

Professional
Tips

GOING ON AUDITIONS

Auditions (or tryouts) are job interviews for actors. Look below for what to do, how to dress, how to act, what to ask, and what to bring on an audition.

What to Do if You're Nervous

- Breathe.

- Laugh.

- Squinch up your face and body very tight and small, then let everything go loose to relax your muscles.

- Focus on your heart.

What to Wear to an Audition

- Nice, neat clothes

- Not a costume

- Clothes that your character might wear (if your character is from the past, choose something he or she might wear today in modern times)

The Slate

A slate is stating your name and what you will be doing at the start of an audition. For a film, TV, or commercial audition, you will say the slate to the camera. You may also be asked to say the product in the commercial or the part you are auditioning for. For example:

TV/Commercial/Movie Slate: "Hello! My name is Kristen Dabrowski, and I will be auditioning for the role of Jane."

Theater Slate: "Hello! My name is Kristen Dabrowski, and I will be singing a song called 'My Favorite Things.'"

You can show your personality on your slate, but just tell the people watching you the important facts (who you are, what you will be doing).

Professional
Tips

63

Working in Front of a Camera

The director or the casting director (in an audition) will tell you where to look. If you have a scene with another person (or people), you will almost always look at the other actors when they speak or when you speak to them. If you are told to look at the camera, there is usually a little red light on the top of the camera you can look at. If you don't see a red light, look at the lens. Pretend the camera is another person. The friendlier and more relaxed you are with the camera, the better.

Who Is There

In an audition, sometimes your mother or father may be allowed to go in with you. Other times, you may be asked to go in by yourself. If this is something that scares you, you may want to wait until you're older to be an actor. Once you walk into the audition room, they will probably talk to you for a minute or two, asking simple questions. The questions are not a test of how much you know! They are to see what your personality is like and whether you are able to speak confidently.

What to Ask

In an audition or with a job, sometimes a good question to ask is, "How much of me is seen?" Sometimes the camera is only focused on your face, other times it shows your whole body. This can change your acting a little bit. When the camera is up close, actors should behave naturally (unless the director tells you not to). Also, when the camera is up close (called a close-up), if you move around too much, you'll go in and out of the frame (what the camera sees). Generally, you should stay pretty still during a close-up.

The more of your body the camera shows, the more free you can be with your body to move around. If a camera shows the whole room, the director will give you *blocking*. Blocking is where you move and when. Just like a dancer being told what moves to do, an actor is given blocking. For example, the director may say, "When you say, 'I gotta go,' walk to the door." It's usually pretty simple, but it's important to remember it and get it right.

If you are confused about what something in the script means, always ask. Also, if you aren't sure how your character feels, ask that, too! The director will be happy to explain for you. Always ask if there is something you don't understand. Don't be embarrassed about that. Everyone wants you to do well, and they want to help you!

Professional
Tips

64

Pictures

Professional actors get a big photo taken of them to take to auditions, called a headshot. Why? So when you leave the room, the people watching you (directors or casting directors) can remember who you are and what you look like. Sometimes directors and casting directors see *hundreds* of actors a day!

- Your picture should be 8 by 10 inches (if you can't get a professional photographer to take your picture, you can just bring in a regular picture until you can afford it).

- Your picture should look like you. Not like you with a lot of makeup on or like you after you've spent two hours doing your hair. It shouldn't look older than you or younger than you. It should look like *you*. The photo helps the directors remember you. If your picture doesn't look like you, no one will recognize your photo and know who to call if you get the job!

For kids, people usually don't mind if your picture isn't taken by a professional photographer. Since children's looks change a lot as they grow, it's more important that the photo looks like you. So having a picture taken by a friend or a relative is OK.

Sometimes an actor will have two different pictures, a happier pose for commercial work and a more serious-looking one for dramatic work.

Note: In "Interviews with Actors and Agents," you can take a peek at two actors' 8-by-10 headshots (see pages 80 and 90).

Résumés

A résumé is a list of your important information, your acting experience, and your special talents.

- **Important information.** Your name, your telephone number, your weight, your height, the color of your hair and eyes.

- **Acting experience.** As a young person, you may not have much acting experience. That's OK! If you were in a school play or modeling show or anything else, write it down. If you sing in the school choir or take acting classes, write it down. Anything that has to do with acting.

- **Special skills.** Can you do anything unique? Play the oboe, sneeze on cue, do karate? Add that to the end of your résumé.

Note: In "Interviews with Actors and Agents," you can take a peek at two actors' résumés (see pages 89 and 101).

Professional
Tips

WHAT IS AN ACTOR'S DAY LIKE?

When you are an actor, sometimes every day is different. Unlike some other jobs, you don't always go to the same place every day, and most jobs do not last for years and years. Here are some ways an actor's day can go:

Looking for Work

Lots of times, actors have to go to auditions and look for work. They also do mailings to agents and casting directors—people who can help get them auditions and jobs. A mailing contains:

- The actor's picture

- The actor's résumé

- A short cover letter to the person the actor is writing to

There are a few newspapers, websites and other publications with news about jobs for actors. The most important ones are:

- *Backstage*

- *Ross Reports* (a list of agents, casting directors, and the movies/TV shows being made)

- *Show Business*

These papers mostly include jobs, agents, etc., in major cities, but some information for other places can also be found.

Warning! No agent, casting director, or manager should EVER ask you for money unless he or she helped you get paying work. Anyone who asks you for money before he or she helped you get work is not a person to be trusted.

Cover Letters

Cover letters are addressed to agents, casting directors, and, sometimes, producers and managers. Cover letters should be simple. Say who you are, why you are writing, and a little bit about your acting experience (especially any new acting work). If you are writing a casting director to try to get an

Professional
Tips

66

exact job, you might write one or two sentences about why you would be right for that part. For example, if a casting director is looking for someone who sounds like they are from Texas, and you *are* from Texas, that would be something to include!

On the Job

On a film, TV, or commercial job, expect to wait around a lot. There are a lot of lights and cameras to set up. They will bring you clothes to wear and do your hair and makeup. Sometimes with kids, there's no makeup at all. There's food on the set (called kraft services). You will get breaks. Ask for what you need (like a drink of water when you're thirsty or a minute to think if you get mixed up), but always be polite and nice to everyone. When you are nice to work with, people want to work with you again!

Under the Lights

It is very hot under the lights. Don't squint or complain. Get used to it. Lights are always bright, and all actors get used to them.

Working with Microphones

When you work with a microphone, recording just your voice, it's called a voice-over. Voice-overs are used in commercials and cartoons—any time you don't see an actor's face but you hear voices. When you speak into a microphone, you want to get pretty close to it, and you don't need to yell. The more you can relax and have fun, the better!

Getting the Job!

Getting the job is great! Actors need to check their schedules to see if they can make all performances and rehearsals (practice times).

Not Getting the Job!

No actor in the whole wide world gets every job he auditions for. In fact, an actor usually needs to go on a whole bunch of auditions before she gets a job. Just think "oh well!" and try again another day.

Professional
Tips

67

Why Didn't I Get a Job?

Don't worry about why you didn't get a job. Often, it's because of something silly, like you were too tall or the person playing the mother has brown hair and your hair is red. It's almost never because you did a really bad job.

Rehearsing

Here are some important rules for rehearsing (practicing):

Listen to the director.

Try new things, as long as they make sense.

Focus and pay attention.

Have fun!

Having Fun Versus Being Serious

Always pay attention at a rehearsal and be in character. But that doesn't mean you should be serious all the time! When you are taking a break, you can act as goofy as you want. Don't get mad at yourself or someone else if things don't go exactly right. Have a good attitude and a sense of humor about yourself.

If your character is silly, can you be silly? Of course!

Professional
Tips

PARENT TIPS

Parents, here are some very important tips:

- Make sure your child enjoys performing.

- Ask your child how classes or auditions are going; listen closely to his responses.

- If she doesn't like going to auditions, you may want to let her continue with school plays and community activities. Let *her* decide if it's time to become a professional and let *her* decide at any time when it's time to stop.

- If your child doesn't like going to his class, find a new class. Most communities have a lot of offerings; it may just be that your child's class isn't a good fit.

- Never, ever pay an agent or a manager if he or she does not get your child paying work. Agents and managers usually take about 10 percent from an actor's earnings *after* the actor gets paid.

- Be a good audience.

- Be encouraging. Encourage your child to ask questions when she doesn't understand another person's ideas or choices rather than saying she doesn't like something. (This is a good tip for adults, too.)

- Be a mind-reader. As much as you can, figure out what your child needs to hear. Is he hoping for praise and encouragement or is he open to hearing some suggestions? The difference between a hurtful comment and a good idea often comes down to having an upbeat tone of voice and a light-hearted approach.

- Know when it's too much. Acting, especially for kids, should be fun and not stressful. If all the fun is getting sucked out of it, it's time to pull back and relax a little.

- Use *your* imagination!

- Show your child new exercises and games. Acting games can be a great way to build self-esteem, foster creativity, and find out what your child is thinking and feeling.

Professional
Tips

- Read scenes and monologues for kids with your child. Talk about what you are reading. *My First Scene Book* and *My Second Scene Book* have great discussion questions. All the books in *My First Acting Series* are interactive.

- Get involved! Watch your child perform.

Professional
Tips

GAMES

Try these games!

What emotion is this girl showing?

WORD FIND!

```
H C A M E R A N O I T I D U A P
A O A S Y A L P B S E N S E S R
P M S C J O Y T V S H O W U F E
P M M R T R E T I R E B T N M T
T E E I P R E H E A R S A L O E
O R L P O P E U N E E E S I N N
U C L T R H F S Z S S R T N O D
C I C T P O S I U A E V E E L N
H A O E E T R J G M T E C S O O
A L S O N O I R O Y E N C I G I
P T T A M A K E U P D E E N U T
O Z U E E C N A D A N I F G E O
I I M P R O V C M E L V U N M M
G R E T A E H T A U S O N G A E
X S A D M R E G A N A M K K E E
B E L I E V E G E C I T C A R P
A D B E Y O U R S E L F R A D T
```

Find and circle the acting words below in the puzzle. They may be horizontal, vertical, diagonal, or backwards. This is a difficult word find! Take your time and look closely. Find the secret message!

Actor	Dream	Manager	Pretend	Prop	Set
Actress	Emotion	Memorize	Prop	React	Sing
Agent	Fun	Monologue	React	Rehearsal	Smell
Audition	Hear	Movie	Rehearsal	Resume	Song
Believe	Improv	Observe	Resume	Sad	Taste
Camera	Joy	Photo	Play	Scene	Theater
Commercial	Lines	Play	Plot	Script	Touch
Costume	Mad	Plot	Practice	See	TV Show
Dance	Makeup	Practice	Pretend	Senses	

CONNECT THE DOTS

Connect the dots from 1 to 30 and see what costume this boy is wearing.

Hints:

He is going to MARCH in the Halloween parade.

He doesn't care if it is COLD.

He hopes there are FISH sticks for lunch today.

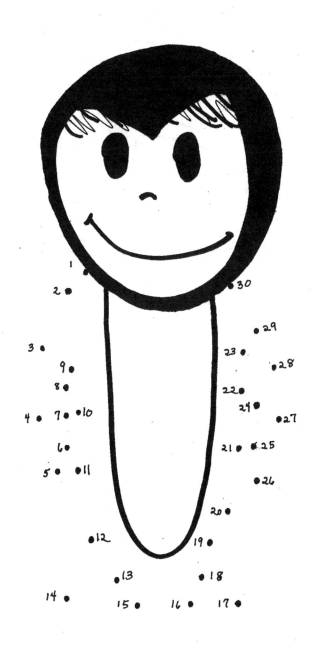

Games

73

AN ACTOR'S DAY MAZE

Take this path:

HOME ➤ AGENT ➤ REHEARSAL ➤ AUDITION ➤
(back to) REHEARSAL ➤ CLASS ➤ HOME

Games

84

AN ACTOR'S LIFE PENNY GAME

1. Get a penny and flip it in the air.

2. If it lands on heads, move forward two spaces.

3. If it lands on tails, move forward one space.

4. Keep going around the track until you get at least one job!

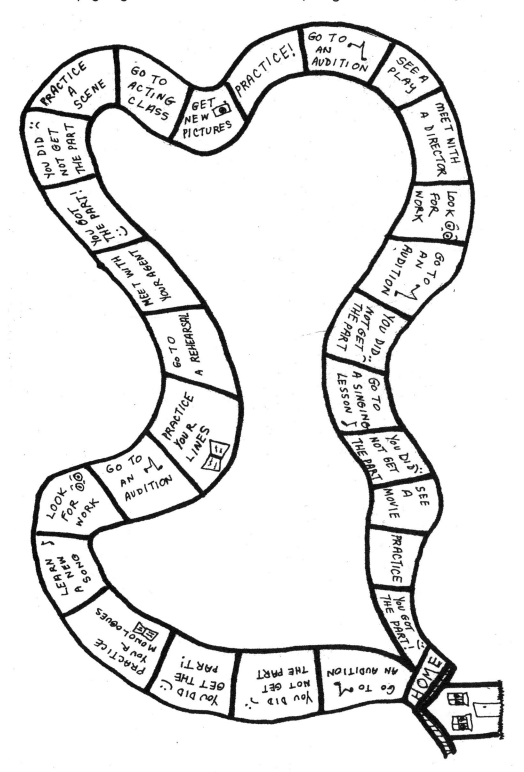

Games

75

COSTUME DESIGNER

Choose the costumes you like best and put them on the boy and girl. Or make them try on all the costumes! (You can also make your own costumes for them.) And for goodness sake, give them some hair and shoes!

Games

Games

77

SHOW THE EMOTION

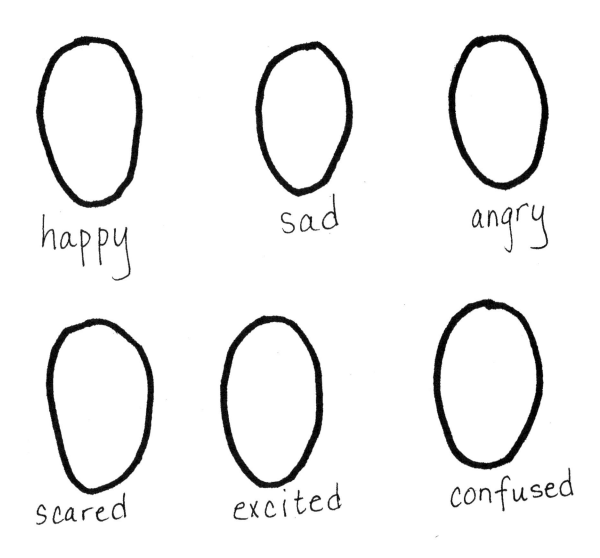

happy   sad   angry

scared   excited   confused

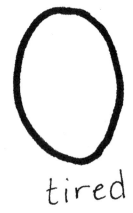

surprised   tired

Games

78

INTERVIEWS WITH ACTORS AND AGENTS

Four performers under the age of fourteen tell you what it's like to work as entertainers and two agents give advice on how to get into show business.

What is this boy doing?

INTERVIEW WITH RACHEL COVEY

RACHEL COVEY loves her cat, Miley Cyrus, and spending time with her family and friends. She's ten years old and lives in New York City. Rachel is also an actress. She's been in commercials for Cheerios, Lowe's, and Leap Frog, but she's best known for playing Morgan in the Disney movie *Enchanted*. I met with Rachel and her mother, Dana, to ask them about acting.

How did you get started in acting?

RACHEL: I was really little. When I asked my mom to let me [act], she said no.

So it was your idea [to get into acting]?

RACHEL: It was my idea—yeah! I saw people on TV and thought, "I want to do that."

RACHEL'S MOM: I had been a performer, and I actually held off for a while because I didn't want people to think I was fulfilling my own dreams through my kid. . . . The summer she turned four, there was an ad at a ballet academy saying they wanted a girl to be in a movie. . . . So I thought, you know what, it's a stressless [situation]. In the real deal, you have to mail in pictures and all that; this one she just had to call. They faxed me a monologue for her to learn from the script.

Working on a monologue when you're just four years old? Was it hard to memorize?

RACHEL'S MOM: I read her the lines. She repeated them back to me perfectly. I purposely didn't emote, and she instinctively knew how to deliver the lines. She got a callback, and they sent her yet another very long monologue—even longer, a different one. And she learned that one. She has a very good auditory memory.

RACHEL: What's that?

RACHEL'S MOM: You memorize better by hearing.

RACHEL: Yeah, I so do.

RACHEL'S MOM: They didn't make that movie for a long time; Rachel didn't end up doing it. But they told us we should really call this agent, and the agent was already expecting our call.

RACHEL: Yeah, and I got signed [by the agent] for that. Because of the auditions.

What happened when you went to meet the agent?

RACHEL'S MOM: She went in by herself. She was just four years old.

Were you grown up for a four-year-old?

RACHEL'S MOM: She was tiny, actually.

RACHEL: I was really little. That's how I get a lot of parts. They're looking for small people. 'Cause you can act like a younger kid, but you understand things like an older kid.

Do you remember meeting the agent?

RACHEL: I remember them asking what I like to do. And I said, "I like to draw and stuff." I had no idea what the heck was going on. I didn't get it at all.

RACHEL'S MOM: It's not about how cute your kid is (that helps, obviously). They really want a kid who will go in a room without their parent and who will talk. Because some kids, when they're with strangers, will clam up.

RACHEL: I'm a blabbermouth.

Is it hard or easy to be yourself when you're meeting people—agents and casting directors?

RACHEL: It depends. When I was younger, it was easier. Now sometimes I feel like I have to act more mature; sometimes it can be hard to be yourself. But you have to be yourself because they want to see if you're someone they're gonna want to work with.

There's a lot of times when you don't get jobs, isn't there?

RACHEL: A lot of times you can really get your hopes up.

RACHEL'S MOM: I explained to her that in commercials they're creating a family—matching a mommy and a daddy and a little girl. Do you look like the parent?

RACHEL: Sometimes you can be great, but you don't look like the mom they picked. You really don't know how it's going to go. Sometimes you go to an audition, like when I went to audition for *Enchanted*, and you think, "Oh my gosh, that was terrible," and then you get the part. You really don't know.

Do you try not to think about whether you got the part after you audition?

RACHEL: I usually try not to think about it because if you get your hopes up and you don't get it, it's really sad. The good news when you get a part is that you got the part! The bad news is that there are scripts to learn, and you're gonna miss parties. So we try to look at good news/bad news. That makes it easier if you don't get the part.

How do kids at school treat you?

RACHEL: I told my friends, "Guess what? I'm going to be in a movie!" And when it came out (two years later), my friends didn't treat me that different because we're friends. But older kids would stop me and say, "Excuse me, I think I know you from somewhere." It was weird, but it died down after a while.

Do your friends ever get jealous?

RACHEL: I don't think my friends get jealous, a friend is a friend, and you can tell. But sometimes I have a case where things don't start out so great with someone, then they'll find out about my acting, and they'll want to be my best friend. It's hard. You have to be able to see through people and see if they like me because I act or because of me.

What is it like when people stop you on the street?

RACHEL: It's really scary sometimes. Why me of all people? I'm still a normal person. Randomly people start talking to me. They know me, and I don't know them. It can be scary sometimes.

Are you in and out of school a lot for auditions?

RACHEL: School comes first, definitely. You can't be a famous dumb person.

RACHEL'S MOM: Rachel just auditions for things filming near home.

RACHEL: I have a brother. If I went to Hollywood to make a movie, it would mess up everybody's life. That's not right. [The work] has to be appropriate, too. Bad language and stuff like that, I won't do.

RACHEL'S MOM: If she doesn't (or we don't) feel comfortable, then she doesn't do it.

When you're acting, you have to show emotions. In *Enchanted*, you had to cry. How did you do that?

RACHEL: Usually, you just think of something sad, put yourself in the character's shoes. But for me, we filmed the crying scene last. So I was thinking, "I'm going to miss all these people and filming." That itself made me teary.

RACHEL'S MOM: Sometimes I say, "Can you imagine what it would be like to be in this character's situation?" Or other times I'll tell her to imagine what it would be like if someone took her cat.

RACHEL: Ooooh!

RACHEL'S MOM: That always works. Or if she has to be really mad, she'll think of a time when her brother was mean to the cat.

Do you like having your mom help you with your acting?

RACHEL: But sometimes it's easier to have my mom helping me out. I feel more comfortable. But it's funny sometimes when I have to be really mad, and I practice with my mom, and I have to scream at her. I can't do it!

If you woke up next year, and you didn't want to do it any more, would you just quit?

RACHEL: Yeah. Lots of times, you have stage moms telling kids they have to do it, win the part. But acting was my idea in this case. My dad always says, "If you don't wanna do it, don't do it."

RACHEL'S MOM: I always ask her. I say, "There's an audition, but if you don't want to go, you don't have to."

RACHEL: If there's something else going on, we'll try to reschedule it for another day. Sometimes there will be a really cool audition, but my best friend and me—I don't get to see her a lot. Acting is not as important. It's not my entire life. It's fun for me, but your own life comes first.

How often do you go to auditions?

RACHEL'S MOM: We try to be flexible. Sometimes there could be two or three auditions a week, sometimes there's a month with nothing.

RACHEL: Sometimes it can be every day a week! And sometimes, nothing for a year. Well, I'm exaggerating a little.

What's the difference between film audition and commercial auditions?

RACHEL: For film auditions, they'll usually send you a script that you have to rehearse in advance. When you have a film audition you have to be more serious and show that you can do it. In commercials, they give you the lines when you get to the audition. They say, "Tell me your name and how old you are, then pretend that there's two different cups of yogurt in front of you. Pick the one that looks more delicious." I personally have no real favorite.

RACHEL'S MOM: You often have to wait around longer in a commercial audition, but, with films, you have an exact appointment time.

RACHEL: Or for a voice audition, like animation, you have to really show them your acting with your voice, not your facial expressions. They'll have you say things a lot of times, in different ways.

What do you think makes you a good actress?

RACHEL: I think it's about putting yourself in the character's shoes. Then you can really get into it.

RACHEL'S MOM: I think with kids, they want to find the kid who is the closest in real life to the character.

RACHEL: You have to really get into it if the character isn't like you. That can be hard.

RACHEL'S MOM: In *Enchanted*, they were looking for a kid who really believed.

RACHEL: Morgan is a kid who believes in fairy tales. They asked me if anything like a fairy tale had ever happened to me. Well, I remember this one time—this is actually true—I was awake when the tooth fairy came. I was fake-sleeping, and I heard this sound—this is a true story!—I heard her under my pillow, and then she flew away. . . They probably thought, "This girl believes, just like Morgan." So if you can be the character, that helps.

Do you do mailings?

RACHEL'S MOM: No. Once you have an agent you don't have too. Plus, Rachel didn't get a headshot [an acting picture] until about a year and a half ago.

RACHEL: Before, we'd just take a picture on the digital camera and print it out.

RACHEL'S MOM: Kids change so much. We'd just take a new picture every six months or so, print it out, make a photocopy and blow it out to 8-by-10 size.

RACHEL: They [agents and casting directors] don't always like the people who are all fancy-schmancy. You can be just another person who also happens to like acting. They like the people who are real, not fake; they go to school, plus they can act. I don't wanna be a person who barely has an education and during my whole childhood never had time for my friends. Acting doesn't make you special. It's like a hobby. Just being yourself makes you special.

When you do a film, there's a lot of waiting around. What do you do?

RACHEL: Yeah. Everyone else, they lay around, relaxing. Me, I have to do my math homework.

You have a tutor teaching you when you work on movies. Is that easier than being in regular school?

RACHEL: It's not. I had to do three hours of school work a day. So I had to play Morgan, then do my math. Talk to Giselle [another character in *Enchanted*], do my spelling. It was literally chaos.

I bet a lot of kids would think three hours of school would be easy, instead of going to school all day.

RACHEL: It's actually hard. It's hard to focus. Sometimes you wish you could be an adult and relax. You have to get in all your schoolwork; it's the law.

RACHEL'S MOM: Sometimes you can work all day until six o'clock and still have to wait and stay so you can finish your homework.

Is it hard to have a regular life when you're making a movie?

RACHEL: I was supposed to have my birthday party when we were doing *Enchanted*, and it was, basically, the most important thing in the world to me. We asked them to let me have a day off to do that (and they did). It's important to keep doing regular things. It can be hard, but you have to try.

What do you like best about acting?

RACHEL: I like when I get the part!

If you were going to give someone advice who wanted to start acting, what would you tell them?

RACHEL: You can't always assume a character's personality. Sometimes you act happy and they say, "This character has a very dry personality." So you have to do it again and again, but you can't get frustrated. I think it's a lot about patience. You can't get mad.

RACHEL'S MOM: And you shouldn't feel bad about asking questions.

What's your advice, Dana, for parents who are thinking of getting their kids into show business?

RACHEL'S MOM: It's a business. It's hard for kids to understand that, but parents need to. Most decisions are based on it being a business.

Do you think acting helps or hurts your self-esteem?

RACHEL'S MOM: Most kids who act have good self-esteem. But you are opening yourself up to people volunteering their opinions of you.

When you're older, do you think you'll want to go to Hollywood and be in movies?

RACHEL: When I'm older, I think I might want to do auditions like that, when I'm ready. But right now, I'm still a kid, I'm still in school, and I still like being with my family.

Do you think you'll always be an actor?

RACHEL: I'm never going to quit. I love, really love acting. There are ups and downs, but I know when I grow up I'm going to keep doing it. When I'm a million years old, I'll probably retire.

RACHEL COVEY
S.A.G.

Height: 54 ins.
Weight: 68 lbs.
Eyes: Green/hazel
Hair: Light brown

[Agent name and phone number]
[Home phone number]
[Mom's cell phone number]

Film

Enchanted	Morgan (principal)	Disney; Kevin Lima, Dir.
Duane Hopwood	Kate (supporting)	Blue Magic Pictures/ Evolution Filmworks; Matt Mulhern, Dir.

Television

30 Rock	"Stage Manager"	NBC

Commercials
Several national commercials, including Cheerios, Loews,
Duncan Hines, and more (list available upon request)

Special Skills
Singing, tennis, swimming, rollerblading, ice skating, Heelys
Plays piano (studying for four years)
Can raise one eyebrow at a time and wiggle ears

INTERVIEW WITH
MATTHEW LOBENHOFER

MATTHEW LOBENHOFER is a triple-threat: he is an actor, a singer, and a dancer. He performed alongside star Patti LuPone in the Broadway musical *Gypsy*. Matthew lives in New York City with his mom, his dad, and his older sister, Emma. Fortunately, Matthew and his mom, Angie, found a few minutes to talk to me about being in show business.

How old are you, Matthew?

MATTHEW: I'm twelve.

And you were in *Gypsy* on Broadway. Was that your first show?

MATTHEW: It was my first Broadway show, yeah.

How long have you been acting?

MATTHEW: I've been acting since I was about four or five, in school plays and stuff.

So you've been acting for almost your whole life?

MATTHEW: Yeah.

You just had a tap class. You take classes all the time, don't you?

MATTHEW: Yeah, I do.

What do you take classes in?

MATTHEW: I take ballet, tap; I used to take West African [dance], acting, singing, hip-hop. I take a *lot* of classes.

You're what we would call a triple-threat. You act, sing, and dance. What's your favorite thing to do?

MATTHEW: Act.

What do you like about it?

MATTHEW: Being different people, but having a little bit of me in it.

So your favorite thing about being an actor is playing different characters. Why do you like that?

MATTHEW: I don't know, I guess I just like to learn about other people and other people's lives. I know my life, I know how my life goes. Maybe it changes a little, but I even know those changes. The reading was about a boy; he lived next to the Twin Towers when they fell. It was cool learning about that. In *Gypsy*, it was fun learning about people in vaudeville [a type of entertainment performed from the 1880s to the 1930s].

You go to a special school.

MATTHEW: Yes. The Professional Performing Arts School [PPAS].

How is that different from going to a regular school?

MATTHEW: Well, a lot of the kids understand you more because other kids—If you say, "I have an audition," they say, "Oh, what for? What show are you doing?" We compare dance classes; we take each other's dance classes. This school has singing, acting, dancing, instead of PE and some other things.

How long do you take academic classes and how long do you take performing classes?

MATTHEW: We have four periods in the morning of . . . academic stuff, then we have an hour and a half of singing or dancing or acting. We have acting three times a week, singing twice, and dancing once.

So you take English, Social Studies . . .

MATTHEW: . . . math and science.

That's four academic classes. I bet a lot of kids would be jealous of that.

MATTHEW: I bet!

When you were in *Gypsy*, you didn't go to a school at all, did you?

MATTHEW: I did. I went to the school I'm going to now, and I also went to The Professional Children's School. It's pretty much the same kind of place as the school I'm going to now, but it's a private school. I ended up going to PPAS because it's closer to the subway I have to take.

Did you ever have to have a tutor instead of going to school?

MATTHEW: In rehearsals. We had two tutors, Rachel and Leona. They were really good.

You have to be in rehearsals all day.

MATTHEW: Yeah, all day. Six days a week.

Was it hard to get your work done?

MATTHEW: Yeah. It was. Since we [the Newsboys] were only on for, like, forty-five minutes of the show (the show is three hours), we just did homework backstage. It's really hard, though, because a lot of the kids were homeschooled so they were allowed to do their homework at home. And they would just play or do whatever backstage while I had to do homework.

So it was hard to concentrate?

MATTHEW: Yeah, but sometimes I'd just say, "why not," and just play. I'd leave the rest [of my homework] for at home later.

Do you also have to listen to what's happening onstage when you are waiting in your dressing room?

MATTHEW: You can adjust the volume, but the wrangler [a person who keeps track of children backstage] liked to have it on so she would know where we were [in the show].

That must make it hard to concentrate, too.

MATTHEW: Sometimes, like when this character Tessie Tura was onstage, I'd be writing [for my homework], then all of a sudden, I'd look back to read it over and it says, "The boy went over the bridge to see Tessie Tura." And I'd think, "How did that get there?"

When you were performing on Broadway, your nights were really long, weren't they?

MATTHEW: I'd get out [of the show] around eleven, then I'd have to change out of my costume, and *then* it took about an hour or forty-five minutes to get home. So then I'd take a shower and try to fall asleep.

When did you have to get up in the morning to go to school?

MATTHEW: Probably 6:50.

So you'd get about six hours of sleep. I love sleep. That sounds awful!

MATTHEW: I know! Like now, I go to sleep, and I'm so happy.

Are you doing auditions now, since *Gypsy* is over?

MATTHEW: Yeah, I'm still auditioning. I just finished a reading [when actors act out a play without costumes or sets for the playwright and producers to see if people like it]. I don't know if I have more auditions coming up, but I am auditioning.

Interviews
with Actors
and Agents

94

You're twelve. Do you get cast as a twelve-year-old?

MATTHEW: Usually not. Like the reading, I was supposed to be 10. In *Gypsy*, the actors were aged ten to thirteen, but we were supposed to be short.

When I was talking to Rachel Covey, she thought being shorter was an advantage for her as an actor. She looked younger, but she could act more mature. Do you think that has helped you get some parts?

MATTHEW: Yeah, except now I'm getting into a phase where I'm growing.

I'm glad you brought that up. You are getting taller. What is that like? Is that something that worries you?

MATTHEW: The parts I want, a lot of them, are for my age. But since I'm about to be out of my age, and I'm getting taller, it's kind of disappointing to see that I have one last chance [for those parts], and then maybe it's over. Maybe I get it, but you don't really know.

But it's not something you can help, getting taller!

MATTHEW: Kind of. If you had iron bars in your head, holding you short while you sleep, maybe you wouldn't grow.

That's crazy!

MATTHEW: [Laughs.]

Your father said that it was in your contract that you can't gain weight either.

MATTHEW: I had to stay within ten pounds of my weight. Sometimes I would have a growth spurt, and I'd eat a lot and get heavier. And I'd have to work it off. Luckily, it's not too hard to stay within ten pounds.
[*Note:* I should say that Matthew is very fit. The weight and height rules are more about looking a certain age. There's nothing wrong as an actor with being taller or bigger as long as you look right for the part you are playing.]

You've done mostly plays, right?

MATTHEW: Yeah. Plays and musicals. I've never really done a movie. Well, I did a computer movie called *The West Side*. It's kind of like a modern-day Western.

What makes being on stage fun?

MATTHEW: Seeing the audience.

Do you think that being a stage actor is what you want to do?

MATTHEW: Yeah. Either that, sports, or martial arts.

I was just about to ask you: If you didn't do acting, what would you do?

MATTHEW: Probably that. I've had a passion since I was about three, about to be four, for tae kwon do. I've been growing in the styles. I like the different styles. But I still like tae kwon do. I still do it. Sports, I just grew up in a sports school. I was kind of forced to like sports, and I guess it worked.

Are you still able to do sports with all the dance classes you take?

MATTHEW: Not really. At my school there are no sports programs or anything. In my house, I have a playroom. Not that big. But I have a lot of sports stuff in there. Sometimes I'll take out a soccer ball and dribble it around.

When you were in *Gypsy*, you were around a lot of adult actors who had a lot of experience. Some of them are famous. What was that like?

MATTHEW: Well, it's kind of weird because a lot of them are talking about [acting and acting technique], and you learn from them. Secrets about what you're supposed to do. Like Patti LuPone, I didn't know who she was before this, but as soon as I found out who she was, I knew she was famous. And knowing her, it doesn't really seem like she's famous 'cause people say some famous people are like divas, but she's not a diva at all.

We had jokes with the stagehands and stuff. It was nice because you'd have different relationships with different people. And they're all good relationships.

There were other kids working on your show, too.

MATTHEW: Yeah, six other kids. Two left partway through, so eight actually.

What was that like?

MATTHEW: It's fun. Because I was the only one from New York City. There were two from New Jersey; one from Albany; one from San Antonio, Texas; one from Virginia; one from Connecticut—all over the place. Florida—everywhere.

Do you keep in touch with them?

MATTHEW: Yes, some of them are still here for auditions. A lot of them commute to New York if they can. The person from San Antonio comes in every now and then, the girl from Florida is still here . . . We still keep in touch.

Your older sister is a ballet dancer.

MATTHEW: She does all dance, mostly ballet.

All of your family performs.

MATTHEW: My mom mainly does dancing, my dad does acting and singing, my sister, dancing—and me, I'm a mix.

Do you think that helped you?

MATTHEW: Yes. I never wanted to do ballet. But my parents showed me how . . . The reason I did it is that I was doing a program with ballet, Horton [modern dance], and capoeira. Capoeira is a Brazilian martial arts dance. [Capoeira] got me doing it, but I grew to like the ballet and Horton, too.

Do you have any advice for a kid who wants to do what you do?

MATTHEW: Don't do it because you're supposed to do it. Do it 'cause you want to do it. Follow what you feel like you should do. Don't be bothered by anyone; just keep going. Don't let anyone stop you.

Have you had experiences where you don't get the job?

MATTHEW: Yes.

What is that like?

MATTHEW: I've gotten used to it, but I remember when I first started out, I was always really disappointed in myself, and I wanted to push myself harder to be better. Then I'd get something and be happy. I got *Gypsy*; I got *The Grinch [Who Stole Christmas]*, but I had to turn that down; and I got this reading. I think that's it. I mean, you're not going to get a lot of things. But every now and then you'll get it. It feels good to get something. It makes you feel like you're improving. Not getting it, it's just a bummer. But you just keep going.

How long have you been professionally acting [when you get paid for acting]?

MATTHEW: Since I was ten.

What's the first professional audition you went on?

MATTHEW: I went to an audition for *Billy Elliot* when I was nine.

Do you think you'll be doing acting when you're fifty?

MATTHEW: I could. Well, I can't imagine myself being fifty.

Matthew, do you still have friends who aren't at all in the business?

MATTHEW: Almost everyone from my old school is friends with me. I get together with them, I talk to them, I text them all the time.

Do they treat you any differently now?

MATTHEW: Sometimes they'll bring [acting] up. I'll just say, "OK," and try to bring the conversation back to normal things.

I saw a picture of you with Daniel Radcliffe. You've done some things that are pretty exciting. I bet a lot of kids would want to know about those things.

MATTHEW: I want to be a regular kid, but I like doing what I do. So it's a hard mix. But it's always cool to meet someone like Daniel Radcliffe.

You're my person like that. I'm going to tell everyone now that I got to interview Matthew Lobenhofer. Angie, you're Matthew's mom. What advice do you have for parents?

MATTHEW'S MOM: Be careful what you wish for because if they do get a show, you have no life. Unless you have someone that will take them, but you really need to be there as the parent to make sure everything's OK. You have to learn everything [about show business] to protect your child. Even though the Union's* there to protect them, you have to make sure they're getting enough sleep, getting a good education (if that's what you're into, some parents aren't), and just trying to keep them going. He had a great experience, but Mom and Dad are really tired.

This has been a big part of your life, too, getting Matthew and Emma to their classes, rehearsals, and performances.

MATTHEW'S MOM: Yes. It's a very huge commitment. But our feeling is that we'd like to expose them to as many things as possible. But that's it. We don't want to be Mama Roses [a bossy, pushy stage mother who forces her kids to perform in the musical *Gypsy*] or anything like that. We just want to expose them to as much as possible. But it's a commitment. They have to stick to it, and that's it.

But be careful what you wish for. . . . There are so many parents with children from all over the United States with other siblings in the family—everybody suffers. There are a lot of good things [about professional

* *The primary unions to protect actors are: Actors' Equity (AEA) for stage actors, Screen Actors Guild (SAG) for films/TV, and American Federation of Television and Radio Artists (AFTRA) for radio/TV. Until a child gets a union job, there is no need to join a union.*

acting], but there are a lot of negatives, too. That's what you have to pre-pare for.

Do you think there's any point where you would pull Matthew out of the business?

MATTHEW'S MOM: Absolutely. If he really became upset. If he wasn't having fun. For the families who aren't from New York . . . in order to stay here, they have to hustle to get their kids jobs. You have to afford it. It's expensive. Matt has a real life; he has friends; he has a great life. It wasn't as big a deal for him when *Gypsy* was over. He was kind of ready for it. But other kids have pressure on them. It's a hard time.

Any last words?

MATTHEW'S MOM: It does affect your whole family life and any other children you have. So really think about that. But we're thrilled that we did it, and we'd do it again. Right, Matthew?
MATTHEW: Yep.

MATTHEW LOBENHOFER
A.E.A.

[E-mail address]   Height: 58 ins.
[Phone number]   Weight: 90 lbs.
[Cell phone number]   Eyes: Brown
                                                            Hair: Brown

Broadway
Gypsy with Patti LuPone, Dir. Arthur Laurents   Newsboy   St. James Theatre

New York City
Gypsy, with Patti LuPone, Dir. Arthur Laurents   Newsboy   City Center N.Y.C.
Home Sweet Homeland, Dir. Lynn Taylor Corbett   Frankie   One Spirit Seminary
Gypsy of the Year 2008   Gypsy Skit   New Amsterdam Theater
Broadway Easter Bonnet Competition 2008   Gypsy Skit   Minskoff Theater
Tribeca Film Festival   B'way Kids Care Tribeca Stage
Hamlet   Hamlet   Buckley School
Willie Wonka   Willie Wonka   Buckley School

Film
The West Side (Webbie Award)   Qasim (Lead)   Webcast

Dance
Yorkville Nutcracker   Nutcracker   Dances Patrelle
Romeo and Juliet   Page   A.B.T. at Met. Opera
Petrouchka   Rich boy   A.B.T. at Met. Opera
Giselle (2005, 2006)   Village boy   A.B.T. at Met. Opera

Recordings
Patti LuPone: Gypsy (Broadway cast album)   "Newsboy"
B'way's Greatest Gifts: Carols for a Cure   "Room in My Heart"

Member of Broadway Kids and B'way Kids Care (NY l-New Yorker of the Week)

Training
Alvin Ailey School   Ballet/Horton/Capoiera/Tap/West African
Studio Maestro   Ballet/Tap/Jazz/Modern/Flamenco
Janine and Alex Molinari   Musical Theater/Tap and Acro
Creative Arts Camp   Voice/Dance: Hip-Hop/Jazz/Acting/Percussion
Bob Marks and Peter Saxe   Voice

Special Skills
Tae Kwon Do 8 years (high red belt), Capoeira, Percussion, Juggling, Gymnastics, Sports

INTERVIEW WITH
REYNA AND TEMMA SCHAECHTER

REYNA and TEMMA SCHAECHTER, ages thirteen (Reyna) and nine (Temma), are sisters who perform together as a duo called the Shekhter-tekhter (the Schaechter Daughters). In their act, they sing in Yiddish, a language originally used by Jews in Eastern Europe. Reyna and Temma live in New York City. The Shekhter-tekhter have performed across the United States and in other parts of the world, including France and Australia.

You two are singers and have a group together. How did that start?

REYNA: My father, he's been involved in the theater world and in the Yiddish world for over twenty years, so he has many connections internationally. And Temma and I have been performing for a while, both separately and in a larger group, so he thought it might be a good idea to put a show together starring Temma and me. We've been to Paris and Australia.

TEMMA: First, my brother Daneel and Reyna performed together; then Daneel's voice changed. Then Reyna performed alone with my dad for a few years, doing a different show. Now, we [Reyna and I] are performing together, and I play a lot of the parts that Daneel used to play in the songs he performed with Reyna.

I didn't even know you had a brother. Does he mind that you two perform together now?

REYNA: After his voice changed, he became less and less interested. So Temma inherited his role. I don't think he minds that much. He's into bicycling and basketball.

Is he the oldest?

REYNA: Yes, he's seventeen.

How long have you been doing this act?

REYNA: A little less than a year [with Temma]. My brother and I did it five years ago.

Temma, when you were little, did you watch Daneel and Reyna perform? Did you want to do it, too?

TEMMA: Yeah, I wanted to do everything my older siblings did.

Are there ever days when you don't feel like singing or rehearsing?

REYNA: Any opportunity I get to take the stage, I do it. I love it.
TEMMA: Same with me.

How often do you rehearse?

REYNA: Well, in the beginning, before we had our debut, we were rehearsing intensively for over a month, and every week we'd practice for many hours. By the end of our rehearsal process, we had rehearsed for probably about forty or fifty hours. By then, we knew the repertoire. So every time we have a gig now, we rehearse a few times, a few days; we refresh the songs and the blocking. It's pretty much ingrained in our minds. As long as we go over it a few times, we have it.

How do you practice? Does your dad play the piano?

TEMMA: He plays the piano when we sing. He teaches us the music.

Do you read music?

REYNA: Temma doesn't read music, and I read OK, but I don't sight-sing as well as I'd like to.

So you learn by listening and repetition. Do you sing the same songs for each show?

REYNA: Pretty much. For the most part, we perform the same songs because it's a set one-hour revue called "Our *Zeydas* and *Bubbas* as Children" ("Our Grandfathers and Grandmothers as Children"). If they want a slightly longer performance, my dad will perform some additional numbers after our revue is finished.

Do you have to leave school to perform your shows?

REYNA: For Paris, it was during February break. And for Australia, it was during summer break. We were also in Syracuse for a long weekend in June. That weekend happened to start on my last day of school, so I

missed just a half day. But Temma did miss a day of school for that. We try to coordinate it so we don't miss too much school.

So you just go to a regular school.

REYNA: Public school. I go to Hunter College High School and Temma goes to NEST+m [New Explorations in Science, Technology and Math].

Do you have a lot of homework? Is it hard to do both your practicing and your homework?

REYNA: I'm involved in lots of extracurricular activities—I play the piano, I go to my improv club at school, I'm in the musical this winter, I go to Hebrew school—the list goes on and on. But I manage to pull it all off. There are days I go to bed [very late]. Temma doesn't go to bed that late.

TEMMA: I do most of that stuff, too. We don't really do acting every second, every hour, though. We just practice a lot when we're about to do another performance. I get much more time [to do homework] when we don't have a show to practice.

Do the other kids know that you do this?

TEMMA: Yeah. In my class we were playing this game, Two Truths and a Lie, and I wrote, "I perform all around the world," and everyone knew that was the truth.

When you perform around the world, do you get to sightsee or do you have to perform and go right home?

REYNA: In Syracuse, there wasn't a lot to see, but we got to stay in a very nice hotel. But usually we do get to sightsee: we saw the Eiffel Tower; we went to the zoo in Australia and saw wallabies and kangaroos.

Do you think one of you will ever want to quit performing in your group, or do you think you'll always want to do this?

TEMMA: I'm sure it can happen, but I wouldn't think it would happen for a long time.

REYNA: I plan on doing this for as long as I can, but there will come a time when I'm looking for a job that's going to be stable. I love the theater world, but it is risky to become a professional actress, so I will probably still do it for fun, on the side, but I will try to look for a more stable job.

Interviews
with Actors
and Agents

Do you do other performing outside your group together? Reyna, I know you take acting classes, don't you?

REYNA: This summer, I was in a program called The Atlantic Theater Summer Program. . . . It was very intense. We did a lot of vocal exercises and improvs and scene studying. And I was in an acting class this past year, but right now I'm not enrolled in any acting class.

TEMMA: I was in an acting class in my camp, Creative Arts, and I also performed in a musical at that camp. But I don't think I've been in anything other than that.

REYNA: Rehearsing with our dad is kind of like a singing class.

Is it hard performing as siblings? Do you think it would be easier or harder to perform with someone you don't know as well?

TEMMA: I think it would be equal. It's fun to perform with your sister, and it's probably also fun to perform with someone else.

Do you ever argue?

REYNA: [Laughing.] Yes. We don't argue as much [when we're rehearsing and performing] as we do regularly. . . . But there are times even during rehearsals when we do start arguing.

Do you ever have trouble memorizing?

TEMMA: Well, when my dad was teaching me the songs, I would say, "I don't wanna do it, it's too hard, I can't do it." But my dad said, "You can do it." And the first few times, I wasn't really having trouble, I was just lazy. I didn't really listen to my dad. Then, I learned it.

REYNA: If I hear a song once or twice, I can already sing it without looking at the words. Not totally memorized, but I pick up things very quickly.

Have you ever messed up in a performance?

REYNA: When we were in Syracuse, we were performing outdoors. (This incident wasn't really a case of messing up, more like something that would make it to a blooper film.) We were outside, singing under a covered stage, and above us there was this kind of canopy. It had apparently rained a lot the night before, but we didn't know. So, towards the end of our performance, Temma was in the middle of singing a sad song about a Jewish orphan in Eastern Europe whose entire family had

been killed by the Nazis during the Holocaust, and suddenly, out of nowhere, a bunch of water came pouring down right in front of her. But like they say, "The show must go on," and Temma had to go on singing. And I have to say she did a pretty darn good job.

TEMMA: When we were in Paris (our first performance together doing this show), at the end of the show, I started singing words that were from the beginning of the show instead, and Reyna . . . knew I was wrong, so she sang louder than me. Then I remembered!

REYNA: One more "mess-up" that I can think of is that in the middle of the show I sing a song that is very fast paced with lots of words. It was a song that I had recently learned. So I was singing it, and I realized I messed up the words. I think people who knew the song really well realized it, but it was a pretty subtle mistake.

Your act is special, isn't it? It's special because you're sisters, and it's special because you're kids—what else makes it special?

TEMMA: Well, we do sing in Yiddish. Not the whole world understands Yiddish.

Did you understand the Yiddish language before you started doing your show?

REYNA: We were raised speaking Yiddish. My dad speaks Yiddish to us, and our mom speaks mostly English. She throws in a few Yiddish words. But our dad speaks 100 percent Yiddish to us all the time. We're fluent.

Do you like performing in Yiddish?

REYNA: Yes. I like performing more in English because I know English better. I love performing in Yiddish, but with English I'm just a little more fluent as an actress.

TEMMA: I also like singing in English better, because, first of all, more people in the audience understand what I'm singing. Second of all, I'm more used to singing in English. We've done this performance a number of times, but I perform more often in English.

Who comes to your concerts?

REYNA: My dad has many connections. He knows probably a hundred people from Paris and in the other places we perform. So he sends all those people e-mails, notifying them of our gig. Lots of them come. And

some places where we perform publicize in their own publications, and also in Jewish newspapers and on Jewish radio programs. Eventually [the information] gets pretty spread around, and we get a nice audience.

Are most people adults or children?

REYNA: Most people are adults.

Does it make you nervous to perform in front of adults?

REYNA: With performing in general, I might be a little nervous before it begins because I'm not sure if the audience will be responsive, if they'll laugh at the right times. It kind of has to be a mutual effort for the performance to be at its best. But then, when I see that it's a good audience, and they are laughing and clapping at the right times, it's a lot easier and less nerve-wracking.

Do you get stage fright [when you're VERY scared to go onstage] or do you just get a little nervous?

TEMMA: Of course, we do sometimes get nervous.
REYNA: I don't think we suffer from stage fright.
TEMMA: We're used to having adults in the audience. So we don't really get stage fright.

If a kid came up to you and said, "I want to do what you do," what advice would you give them?

REYNA: Well, I think that Temma and I are very lucky to be doing this, and it's mostly because of our dad. We have him to thank. I could lend them my dad, but that's not realistic. I'm not exactly educated on how to become famous. I would say, keep on trying. If you want to pursue it, try going to college for it.
TEMMA: You should study acting, and you should be good at acting.

When you're performing, what are you doing other than singing?

REYNA: We act, we play off of each other, we have some choreography and staging.

You're really good at looking at each other and reacting to each other. Does that come naturally to you or do you rehearse that?

REYNA: We just do whatever comes naturally.

Who makes up your blocking?

REYNA: Usually my dad. But I think it's a collaborated effort. Temma and I, if we have an idea, we'll tell our dad. And we actually experiment with many different things. We use what works, and we don't use what doesn't work.

Some of the things you sing about are pretty serious, like the Holocaust. Does it upset you to sing sad songs?

TEMMA: Yeah. Sometimes. Like when we were practicing here and two of my aunts were watching us, I was singing the Holocaust song and I felt like crying because it was so sad.

REYNA: Actually, one of the aunts had to leave the room because Temma was doing such a good job and she was tearing up.

Does that happen a lot?

REYNA: We have funny songs and sad songs. People do tear up. But we've never had anyone leave a performance, though.

What's the hardest thing about performing?

REYNA: Probably seeing how fun it is now and knowing in twenty years we won't be doing it anymore. That this opportunity of performing together with my sister is only going to be for a certain amount of time. It's not going to be forever.

TEMMA: Probably when a show ends because I really want to keep going and don't want to stop.

Do you have agents or managers to help you with your singing careers?

REYNA: It's just our dad.

Do you have pictures and résumés that you send out?

REYNA: I have a résumé because I needed one for the school musical. And also for the Atlantic Theater summer program, I needed a résumé and a headshot, so I did that all. I did the résumé, and I took the picture with my phone. None of it was done professionally.
TEMMA: I don't have one.

Do you want to do other kinds of acting, like films or TV shows or Broadway?

REYNA: In my dreams I do! But to do that, you need an agent.
TEMMA: Yeah. A lot of kids of my age would like to. I'll probably just keep trying.

What do you think you want to do for a living when you're older?

REYNA: It has nothing do with acting. I either want to be a journalist or a lawyer.
TEMMA: I've been recently writing a lot, so I would also like to be a writer. And also I've just gotten into science, and I'd like to be a scientist.

What is your favorite part of performing?

TEMMA: I really like practicing. I like when my dad makes us do it over and over again. It's kind of funny because of course you don't want to, but he makes us do it over and over and over and over again. . . . That's the funniest part.

It's good that you can have a sense of humor about it, and you don't get mad at your dad. What's your favorite part?

TEMMA: My favorite part is hearing the audience laugh at the right spots, clap at the right spots. And I love seeing the grins on their faces.
REYNA: My favorite part is the curtain call [when performers come out to bow at the end]. When we all come and bow together and my dad joins us. And you see all the people who have watched the performance, and you see (as Temma says) the grins on their faces. It makes me feel great to see that I've made an audience happy.

INTERVIEW WITH
BONNIE SHUMOFSKY AND NEAL C. ALTMAN

BONNIE SHUMOFSKY and NEAL C. ALTMAN work at Abrams Artists Agency—a talent and literary agency, with principal offices in New York City and Los Angeles. Bonnie is an agent in the Youth Division, and Neal is senior vice president and managing director. Abrams Artists Agency represents clients in most areas of the entertainment industry, including movies, TV, animation, theater, and radio. Their Youth Division is highly regarded in the industry, and the agency represents some of the top young talent in the entertainment community.

What is an agent?

BONNIE: An agent, basically, is someone who creates opportunities for their clients. It's my job to find the best match between my clients [actors] and my buyers.

What's the different between a reputable agent and a nonreputable agent?

BONNIE: Anyone who turns around and starts with the phrase "That'll be $5,000 today" is someone who is not reputable. Of course, agencies get a commission, but that comes after the fact. We don't make any money unless the child makes money. Look for franchised talent agencies that come with a connection to the unions, and we are only allowed to take 10 percent [of the actor's earnings]. It's a little different for print, but if the child does not make money, we don't make any money. Anyone that charges [without getting the actor a job], stay away from.

NEAL: And also, someone whose company has been in the business for a good number of years—that's always a good barometer. Not exclusively, but generally a good barometer. They're generally more reputable than someone who's never been heard of.

BONNIE: Nowadays I'd say there are so many outsources—you can go on the Internet and find a number for the ATA, which is the Association of Talent Agencies, and call them and ask them for a list of reputable agents.

NEAL: You can also go to AFTRA [Associate of Film, Television, and Radio Arts].

Interviews
with Actors
and Agents

What kinds of agents are there?

BONNIE: I do commercial, print, voice-overs; I do animation . . . I've booked several films.

Do you also have agents for theatrical work and live-action films?

BONNIE: Yes, we do. I've been here [at Abrams] for close to twenty years, and I have a counterpart who has been here a year longer than me. She's been doing the theatrical end. We took on another junior agent in that department, so we're dividing it up even more. Usually, the kids start in my area and get some experience with the commercials, the print, the voice-overs, then we move them over to film and TV.

If a kid is interested in being an actor, where should they start?

BONNIE: Well, basically, my suggestion is they can start locally in their area—community theater or maybe go to the Y and take an acting class, get involved after school. With little kids, it's usually just a school play . . . as they get a little bit older, there's more opportunities to get involved in the school theater program. And trying to find an agent. Believe it or not, getting an agent is one of the easier parts of getting in. It's getting the job which is the harder part.

How do you want people to approach you? Do you want them to call you on the phone?

BONNIE: No. What I suggest is—I do take referrals, people who call here and say they were referred by someone [already signed at the agency]. Then the procedure usually is, my assistants will say, "That's wonderful. Send us in the mail a picture and a letter saying who referred you, and as soon as we get it, we will give you a call." I open up all my own mail. I'm like Santa Claus. I get a pile of mail every single day of parents submitting their children, and we look through all of them. I'm always looking for different areas to fill, so I'm always looking for different kids. Sending in your picture, just a snapshot, is a really great way. Cold calling—some people might take your call, you might be lucky, [but] most people will say, "I'm sorry." Some people will accept an e-mail, but I prefer regular mail.

NEAL: A lot of kids won't have much in the way of a résumé, but there's always things about [the] child that would be helpful for us to know. Have they gotten involved in school? Did they take classes at the local Y or at a camp program? The problem that we always have over the years

is: Does the child really want to be in the business? Or does the parent want the child to be in the business? And that's something that Bonnie has to work out in a meeting.

What are you looking for? The cutest kid?

BONNIE: You know what, years ago when I first started, there was a certain cookie-cutter look that you had to be. Nowadays, I think the advertiser realizes that everyone eats Oreo cookies and everyone goes to Micky D's and everyone has to buy a car and go on vacation. So the looks have changed. Everyone asks me, "What is it?" And it's just something . . . you just know. You look at a picture, and you see something that jumps out at you . . . And when the kid comes in, it really depends on the age. When a child is between three and, I'd say, six, it's whether the child will make the separation from the parent. Will they come in without the parent? Then it's the poise and the creativity. I want a kid who is going to, when I say, "Hi. How are you?," he is going to say "fine," then start asking me questions. And start telling me things about himself, rather than me having to keep on interacting and asking him . . . Granted, sometimes it is a look. Sometimes you have two parents [actors hired], and you have everything set, and you just need a kid to sit on the couch who is blonde or a certain ethnicity. Then they're going to get the job [based on looks]. But mostly it is a kid who is going to be a chatterbox or have poise and something unique about them. When they're seven to eleven, it's more about their reading skills. That's when it comes into play. Usually I'll give the kid a cold copy [like a commercial to read on the spot] and see how they read the copy and how [well they enunciate] the product [name]. Then, fourteen and up, then it's really a skill at that point. Will I take a beginner? Absolutely. Because sometimes people are a natural. But as they go up [in age], the skill requirements are a little bit different.

When you say reading, you don't just mean the ability to read. You also mean the ability to bring across their personality and the style of what they're reading.

BONNIE: Yup. I'll tell a child, "Slow down, don't read so fast." It's all about expression. If they're little, and they're not sure the first time how to read it, I will go over the directions with them and see if they can give it back to me, because if you're on set and a director says, "Do it this way," and they don't know how to change [their performance to what the director wants], that's a problem.

Interviews
with Actors
and Agents

113

What are some do's and don'ts for parents?

BONNIE: When I find a kid, as much as I love a child and want to work with that child, I think it becomes a complete package . . . The child has to want this. If I can tell the parent wants this [and the child doesn't], that's not something I want to get involved with. The parents need to make sure that the child's education is there—that is very important. That comes before anything. We work around school tests, we work around birthday parties, but the parent has to make sure someone [is available] to bring the child in [to auditions]. If both parents work, and I start calling you for auditions, there better be a grandma or a grandpa or a nanny who can bring the child in. I need a package—a parent I can work with, because I'm not speaking to the kid every day; I'm speaking to the parent.

NEAL: Bonnie's very good about discussing with parents up front at the initial interview. After she speaks with the child, she'll always spend time with the parent. This is something we take very seriously. When we call you with an opportunity to audition, we don't necessarily have the [luxury] of time to wait for you to figure things out. We need to know that you're planning how you're going to get this done. Most times, we get the opportunity the day before or sometimes two days before [the audition]. But there are times when, in the morning, we hear about something that same day. We explain that to the parents. We tell them these are the contingencies you'll have to make arrangements for. If they're not ready to make that kind of commitment—to do whatever it takes to make this possible—we're not sure if we can make that same kind of commitment to them and their child.

BONNIE: I say to parents that it's just like you going to work: [if] you can't make it, you have to call your boss. If you're going out of town, if you're going on vacation—you have to tell me those things, so I don't submit you, and a casting director's interested, and you go, "Oh, well, we decided we're going to Hawaii on Friday." I have to know you're entire calendar. If you have other children, you have to make sure that you can work this around [them]. I tell parents, even if you want to sign with me when you leave my office, go think about it. Call me in a day or two; it's not as easy [a decision] as it seems. As your child gets better and better and does more and more, your lifestyle is going to change. You might have to go to LA for something or go to Vancouver for six months. Are you going to be able to pick up and leave your family and just go?

What shouldn't young actors depend on agents to do for them?

BONNIE: Don't rely on me to get you the job. Like I said before, we create

the opportunity. When someone asks me, "What is an agent?," I kind of describe it as a headhunter [someone who finds people jobs]. A headhunter gets to know you, gets to know where you'll be a perfect match, then sends you out on different job interviews. But then you, yourself, have to sell yourself to the client. I tell my actors that I will create the opportunities for you, but I don't know what you're going to do in the [audition] room when you get there. Just because I'm calling you to go on an audition doesn't mean you got the job. I don't have the time to go over scripts with kids, so don't rely on me to sit down with your child for half an hour to go over it. I would love to help you out, but that's not in my job responsibilities. That's the job of an acting coach, or a manager might help you with that, but that's not the responsibility of an agent.

What should parents spend their money on?

BONNIE: You're going to go on auditions, and you're going to see a nine-month-old with a professional headshot. I just think that is terrible to waste money on. In three weeks, the kid's not going to look like that. Then there are times, around seven or eight, when teeth are falling out or growing in. Nowadays with digital cameras and computers, you can make your own headshot. But I think it's OK for parents to spend money on professional headshots if they want it. Again, do your research. There are a lot of scams out there and unethical places. Nowadays, I think a headshot should be between $250 and $400. Of course, you can go out and spend a thousand at a reputable place, but it's not necessary. You know, you get what you pay for. I tell parents to go to Kmart or JC Penney, and for $14.95, go get a great picture. Use one from school, and go get it blown up. I think parents should take into account the travel expenses. You're almost creating a business for your child, so just like you would have expenses for a copier or something else, you have expenses out of your child's business. It can help your child learn [about money]. . . . There might be certain wardrobe staples that might be OK to spend money on. I'm not saying a parent has to go out and buy a whole new wardrobe, but certain colors jump out. You might want an audition outfit. There are reputable classes you might want to spend money on. There are some classes that say, "Give us $5,000, we'll hook you up with an agent, find you a manager." Don't spend any money like that.

NEAL: Be wary of anyone who ever promises you anything.

What do children do when they come to see you?

BONNIE: Well, what happens with me is that parents check in, an assistant

greets them so they know who the child will be spending time with, then the child comes back to see me. I leave the parents out there because I've noticed that if you bring the parent in for the initial reading, the child always tends to look at the parent and says, "Mom, do I like that?" When kids go on auditions or they go on a set, the parents are within eyesight, but farther away. If they're a certain age, I talk to them and make sure they can talk to me. . . . I might give them cold copy and a moment to rehearse it. Once in a while, they'll ask if they can do a monologue or sing a song; if I see that they're going to be disappointed [if they don't do it] and I have time, [I'll agree to it] . . . But I really don't have the kids prepare anything. I like them to be natural because I find that's what works. The kids that come in and say, "Hi, Miss Bonnie, my name is Kenny, and I'm six years old, and I'm from North Carolina"—that's not going to work. That's a little too over-the-top and rehearsed. Being themselves and being natural is what I like. Because if you're on set and a director tells you to do something one way, and you've rehearsed it another way and it's so programmed in your mind . . . a kid that's not natural won't be able to [adjust his performance].

Do you want kids to come to your office in what they would wear to school that day?

BONNIE: Absolutely. Absolutely! I want the real kid. It's funny, because we're in the acting world, and you have to act the part and be someone else, but I want to know who you are. I don't want a costume.

NEAL: Bonnie mentioned that the needs have evolved. What we do is react and respond to what people are looking for. In reality, the commercial business is a very personal medium . . . The most important thing people are looking for now is: Do they believe the person they are seeing? . . . In order for people to be believable, they need to be comfortable with who they are.

BONNIE: Which is why I look for all different types. When my client calls me, one day they want the kid who would be the chess champion, the next day they're looking for a football hero . . . I have to always look for something new and keep that on my roster.

Do some kids grow out of being in show business?

BONNIE: Sure! Maybe every six months I ask [the kids] to stop by. Because maybe there's a kid who's talkative at three who can become very shy and quiet, or a kid who is dynamic at four who at six and a half is not a strong reader. And I say to a parent, "Listen, this is the time to get them into

classes. This is the time to talk to their teacher at school and get them into a more advanced reading program so they get better." If a boy's voice changes, I need to know that. If someone cuts their hair, I need to know that. So being a kid's agent is a little harder than being an adult agent. They're changing all the time! Also, they lose interest. . . . Or their schedule changes. If I think a kid is great, I'll work around their schedule. I have to be flexible; I deal with children.

Do auditions usually happen after school?

BONNIE: By law, yes. The bookings [jobs] can be during school. In California, the rules are a little different; you need a teacher on set 24/7. In New York, you'd need to work three consecutive days in a row before they have a tutor. But all auditions must be after school.

After you sign someone, how should they follow up? Should parents wait until you call them?

BONNIE: Pretty much. I would check in periodically if you haven't heard from me in six months saying, "You signed my child; I haven't heard from you." If your child changes, please call me and tell me they lost a tooth today. Send me a little note in the mail. But, hopefully, you'll be hearing from me right away. Because I have to create the opportunities for you! If there goes a period where you don't hear from me, by all means, call in and check. If I can't speak to you, leave a message with my assistant.

NEAL: E-mail is a great tool to use, especially because there's certain information we need to get. We don't need for them to check in every day . . . But what we do need is issues of availability.

BONNIE: I think with availability, it's easier to hear in writing. . . . If there's a problem or an issue, then I prefer a phone call. Commercials are a fast-paced world. Unfortunately, during the day, we really don't have time to sit on the phone [with parents or children]. But I will return all phone calls by the end of the day.

Is there anything you wish parents or children knew coming into this business?

BONNIE: Don't take anything for granted. They need to know this is a job. As much as it's fun, this is a job. And the parents have to understand that they have a responsibility. If a child books a job, they're booking it for a client, and that client probably invested a couple of hundred thousand dollars, if not more, paying a crew, other cast members, and for the

Interviews
with Actors
and Agents

budget for [the ad] to run on television. So there's a big picture involved . . . It's not as glamorous as they think it is. It's long hours—you could be out in the cold in a bathing suit. You don't sign up with an agent today and be on the cover of a magazine tomorrow.

NEAL: They have to be willing to invest the time, the energy, the resources. They need to know it's a team effort.

BONNIE: And I think they need to worry about their own child. When they start mixing in with other parents, they start listening. It can get them psyched out, and not everyone tells the truth.

What are the reasons one child will get a part and another won't?

BONNIE: It could be anything. It could be that they went into the room and got scared. It could be that the kid did a fantastic job, did nothing wrong, just did not match with the father—the father has brown hair and brown eyes, and the kid has red hair and freckles . . . Number one, first-choice red-headed kid is no longer getting the part. You have to have a tough shell to do this. A lot of little kids think the audition is getting the part . . . I think it's the parents' job to sit down and explain. If a kid is on the baseball team, and there's nine people on the field and fifteen kids, how do you explain to a kid that they're not starting in the game? . . . What I tell kids is, "You didn't get it this time, but don't get discouraged. We're going to keep on sending you out. There's always tomorrow." I deal with children, and as much as I need to be direct, there's also a comfort side.

NEAL: We don't want them to take the rejection personally. But it's difficult because we want them to be themselves [when they audition].

BONNIE: I've gotten calls where people haven't gotten the part because they're too pretty.

NEAL: The reasons that people get a job or don't get a job are so far out of our control; that's something we need to impress upon the kids. All you can control is getting there on time, doing the best you can, be as comfortable as you can, then look ahead to the next opportunity. That's how we measure success. Can we get continue to get opportunities? And especially if we can get someone in to audition the same place more than once, we know that we're on the right track.

BONNIE: Some of this comes down to luck. Being at the right place at the right time. And then I would say 90 percent of it is coming into a room, having confidence, giving the casting director exactly what he needs to show the client. Then it's up to the client to say, "That's the face I want to sell my ad."

GLOSSARY

Action: What a character does to get his or her way. *See also* Working Actions

Agent: An agent finds auditions for actors. He or she also helps actors get paid after they get a job.

Audition: An audition is a tryout for an actor. Usually the actor reads some lines or does a monologue.

Blocking: Blocking is where you move and when.

Callback: When you get called back in for a second (or third or fourth) audition.

Casting Director: A casting director decides which actors get jobs. A casting director can also call actors to come in for auditions.

Character Journey: How a character changes from the beginning to the end of a story; what he or she learns from his or her adventures.

Close-up: When a camera is very near you while filming.

Commitment: Believing in what you are doing with your whole heart and soul.

Costume: What an actor wears in a play, movie, TV show, or commercial.

Cover Letter: A brief letter to an agent or casting director that says who you are, why you are writing, and what acting experience you've had.

Director: A director is in charge of a play or movie. A director is responsible for telling actors where to go and how he or she wants them to behave in a scene.

Headshot: An 8-by-10-inch photo of an actor.

Improv: An improv is a scene you make up as you go, in the moment. "Improv" is short for improvisation.

In the Moment: Paying attention to what is going on *right now.*

Manager: A manager helps actors pick the best jobs. A manager also helps organize actors.

Memorization: Remembering words from a script without looking.

Monologue: An actor's speech with only one person speaking.

Motivation: The reason why you do the things you do.

Objective: What a character wants.

Observation: Paying attention to what you see.

Plot: What a play, movie, or TV show is about; the major events that occur in a story.

Producer: A producer is responsible for raising money for a play, movie TV show, or commercial. Producers also hire people, like directors.

Prop: Something that an actor holds in his or her hand that is not part of a costume or the set (like a ball or a key).

Reading: A preview of a play, TV show, or movie for producers or small audiences. Actors who perform in readings do not need to memorize their lines (they use a script) and often have very little, if any, blocking.

Rehearsal: A time when a monologue, scene, play, movie, TV show, or commercial is practiced.

Relationship: What connects characters to each other (for example, friends, enemies, sisters, brothers).

Research: Looking in books and asking experts for information.

Résumé: A list of your contact information, vital statistics (eye and hair color, height, weight), acting experience, and special skills.

Set: Made-up rooms or places created for a play, movie, TV show, or commercial.

Scene: A part of a play, movie, or TV show with more than one person.

Script: The text (or words) used in a play, movie, TV show, or commercial.

Senses: There are five senses—smell, touch, taste, sight, and sound.

Slate: Stating your name at an audition. For a theatrical audition, you add what you will be performing. For a TV or film audition, you add what role you are auditioning for. For a commercial or voice-over, you add the product you are selling and the number of the recording "take."

Stage Fright: Being *very* afraid to go onstage.

Staying in Character: Behaving like your character at all times while you are performing and rehearsing.

Voice-over: A recording of an actor's voice, usually heard during a commercial or movie.

Warm-ups: Exercises to get your voice and body ready to perform.

Working Actions: Working actions are different ways of moving that can help actors with voices, movements, and feelings. The eight working actions are punching, pressing, floating, wringing, gliding, slashing, dabbing, and flicking.

THE AUTHOR

Kristen Dabrowski is an actress, writer, acting teacher, and director residing in New York City. The actor's life has taken her all over the United States and England. Kristen is a member of Actors' Equity and The Dramatists Guild. Educationally, Kristen has an MFA from The Oxford School of Drama and has worked at Montclair State University, McCarter Theater, Creative Arts, Creative Theater, Young Playwrights, The American Academy of Dramatic Arts, The Dalton School, and The Actors' Institute, teaching acting, voice, dialects, and playwriting. In addition to My First Acting Series, Kristen is the author of eighteen other books published by Smith and Kraus, including *111 Monologues for Middle School Actors,* volumes 1 and 4; *The Ultimate Audition Book for Teens,* volumes 3, 11, and 12; *20 Ten-Minute Plays for Teens*; the Teens Speak series; and the educational 10+ play series (six books, including two volumes for kids). With experience teaching, directing, and performing for students ages five to twenty-one, Kristen's original writings, guides, and exercises are well researched and road tested.